La Vida Rica:
The Latina's Guide to Success

Yrma Rico
and
Nancy Garascia

McGraw-Hill

New York   Chicago   San Francisco   Lisbon   London
Madrid   Mexico City   Milan   New Delhi   San Juan
Seoul   Singapore   Sydney   Toronto

The **McGraw·Hill** Companies

Copyright © 2004 by Yrma Rico and Nancy Garascia. All rights reserved. Printed in the United States of America. Except as permitted under the United States Copyright Act of 1976, no part of this publication may be reproduced or distributed in any form or by any means, or stored in a data base or retrieval system, without prior written permission of the publisher.

1 2 3 4 5 6 7 8 9 0   DOC/DOC   0 9 8 7 6 5 4

ISBN 0-07-142218-8

McGraw-Hill books are available at special discounts to use as premiums and sales promotions, or for use in corporate training programs. For more information, please write to the Director of Special Sales, Professional Publishing, McGraw-Hill, Two Penn Plaza, New York, NY 10121-2298. Or contact your local bookstore.

 This book is printed on recycled, acid-free paper containing a minimum of 50% recycled de-inked paper.

Library of Congress Cataloging-in-Publication Data

Rico, Yrma.
   La vida rica : the Latina's guide to success / by Yrma Rico and
Nancy Garascia.
     p. cm.
Includes bibliographical references.
   ISBN 0-07-142218-8 (alk. paper)
   1. Hispanic American women—Life skills guides. 2. Hispanic American women—Social conditions. 3. Hispanic Americans—Ethnic identity.
4. Self-actualization (Psychology)—Handbooks, manuals, etc. 5. Success—United States—Handbooks, manuals, etc. I. Garascia, Nancy S. II. Title.
   E184.S75R53 2004
   158.1'082—dc22

2003027000

Contents

Acknowledgments		*v*
Chapter 1	*Sí,* Any Latina Can Live Her Dreams	1
Chapter 2	Finding Work That Makes You *Rica*	25
Chapter 3	Be the *Presidente* of Your Own Life	47
Chapter 4	*Palabras Que Seguir:* Words to Lead By	75
Chapter 5	Pathways to Power: Finding Help on Your *Viaje*	99
Chapter 6	How *Mujeres* Can Win	125
Chapter 7	*La Rica* "Look": Acting the Part	151
Chapter 8	Making the Most of Your *Dinero*	168
Chapter 9	Money Isn't Everything	193
For Further Information		213
Index		215

Acknowledgments

*T*hanks to Walter Ulloa, Philip Wilkensen, and Paul Zevnik, for having faith in me . . . and having the foresight to form Entravision, for without them I would not be here today . . . to all the folks that helped me along the way with their advice and support—you are too many to mention . . . to Louis Aguilar, writer for the *Denver Post*, who put me on the front page of the Sunday paper and brought my cowriter to me . . . to my daughters, Diane and Rebecca Rico, for having the "it's your life, Mom" attitude that helped me make the decisions to take on job opportunities even if it meant moving away from their family and friends . . . to my sisters Lydia and Blanca, who don't have a jealous bone on their bodies, and to my girlfriends, who play the game of golf just to enjoy the game . . . to my former assistant, Rosa Saldivar, who was a tremendous help . . . and last but not least to my mother Paula Garcia, whose words will always ring in my mind, *"Aye Dios Mio y ahora para donde vas"* . . . *A todos Gracias*. . . .

My co-author, Nancy Garascia, and I would also like to thank those people, mostly Latinas, whose thoughts and experiences reinforced and expanded on mine in this book. *Muchos gracias* to Raydean Acevedo, Nelida Quintero, Dolores Kunda, Maria Morales-Prieto, Regla Perez Pino, Caroline Pineras, Kathleen Martinez, Mary Ann Padilla, Maria Rodriguez, Christina Torres, Sara Lora, Juanita Chacon, Elisa Garcia, Rosa Carrillo, Emma Sepulveda, Berta Hernandez-

Truyol, Linda Dominguez, Susan Stewart, Maria Christina, Richard Tanner, Louis Barajas, Ysabel Duron, Susana Navarro-Valenti, Kayleen Maya Aviles, and Rocio Saenz. Also, many thanks to those people who were interviewed or consulted for this book whose stories did not end up in its pages. Please know that we are extremely grateful to you for your time.

Finally, Nancy would like to thank those who made *La Vida Rica* possible. To our agent, Linda Konner, a huge debt of gratitude for providing the initial impetus for this book and for shepherding it to a *simpatico* publisher. To our editor at McGraw-Hill, Mary Glenn, thanks for seeing the potential in this book from the very beginning. Thanks, as well, to my mother, Rachel Shepherdson, and my husband, Larry, for understanding that all would be back to normal in the end.

And hugs to Sally Stich and Laura Daily, without whom Yrma Rico and Nancy Garascia would never have met.

1
Sí, Any Latina Can Live Her Dreams

Listen up, *mujeres.* I'm here to tell you that wherever you started out in life, you can have *la vida rica,* the rich life. Even if your parents were poor, you can live in a big house, have nice clothes, drive a fancy car, send your kids to great schools. You can be happy at work, doing a job you love that satisfies your soul. You can take positions of power and be a leader everyone respects. *Sí, tú puedes.* Yes, you can—and you don't even have to win the lottery or marry a rich husband. You can get anywhere you want to go through your own efforts.

How do I know? Because I've made million. Some days it's hard to believe that because of my success in the business world, I can now buy pretty much anything I want. Why is that so hard to believe? I am the daughter of migrant workers, and I've worked twelve-hour days picking cotton and fruit for $4.50 a day. I've lived without running water and toilets. And I know what it's like to have kids laugh at me because my clothes are ragged. Well, look who's laughing now.

> *Because of my success in the business world, I can now buy pretty much anything I want.*
>
> Yrma Rico

But what does my experience mean to you if you *didn't* start out as the daughter of migrant workers? Just this: If I can become a multimillionaire starting where I did, anybody can do it. *Anybody.* And I want to show you how.

People in Denver, where I worked until recently as the general manager of the Spanish-language Univision station, often see me driving down the street in my black Mercedes convertible or BMW. They must think I'm pretty lucky, as a Latina, to be able to buy such a great ride. But luck had nothing to do with it. From childhood, my thought was always that I could do better than I was doing. In fact, I have always believed that if someone else can do something—whatever it is—I can do it too. I've always been able to figure out a way to get the job done.

> *If you want something badly enough, you have to make sacrifices, not excuses.*
>
> Norma Leza, *principal, Worsham Elementary School, Aldine, Texas*

When I was a teenager, I remember picking peaches in the blazing sun and being jealous of the women who were packing them in a building nearby. They got to sit in the shade and use the bathroom whenever they wanted. Both of those things are really important in the San Joaquin Valley in California, where 90 degrees in the summer is considered a cold snap. It didn't take long for me to ask myself, "How can I get there from here?" How can I get from the hot sun into the shade? I watched how the women in the shade were packing the peaches and figured out a way to do it more efficiently. Then, one day after work, I showed the foreman that I could pack peaches faster than any woman there. Who do you think was working in the shade after that?

GETTING FROM HERE TO WHERE?

Since that day in the peach grove I've asked myself that question over and over: "How can I get from here to there?" Don't get me wrong. In the beginning I never thought I'd be the cofounder of a multi-million-dollar company called Entravision that reaches 80 percent of Hispanic households in the country through TV, radio, newspapers, and billboards. After my divorce I was happy just to make enough money to support my two daughters.

> *Live with wolves, and you learn to howl.*
>
> Spanish proverb

But I've always believed that you must be a *jugadora*, a gambler, to succeed in business or life. For me that means always looking for the next chance, the next play. If I felt that making a move would take me in a positive direction, I would do it.

Does that mean I didn't have a grand plan to achieve *la vida rica*? That's exactly what I mean. I never sat down one day and said: Here is where I want to be someday, and these are the steps I must take to get there. I believe that planning too much gets in the way of achieving big things. Many women, especially Latinas, get so focused on checking accomplishments off their plans that they can totally miss an opportunity to skip several steps—and shoot faster toward their goals.

> *You must be a* jugadora, *a gambler, to succeed in business or life.*

Goals are great, but they've got to be flexible and short-term. I know a woman who writes down her goals for the year in a little notebook and then hides the book for a year. Year after year she discovers that many of the goals she wrote down are accomplished by the time she opens the book to write down another year's goals. Something about writing down goals gives our minds permission to pursue them.

> *Latinas are one of the fastest-growing population groups in the nation. From 1990 to 1999 that population grew 51.7 percent to 11 million.*

What you really need to figure out is what *éxito* (success) means to you. For me it was making more money every year—simple as that. Anyone who has lived in poverty will understand: Going the other way, making less income than I did the year before, was simply too scary. But having lots of money may not be as important to you as having the *respeto* (respect) of people whose opinions you value. Or perhaps you want to make the world a better place. Or maybe you simply want to do your best for your family and make sure your children get a terrific start in life.

Don't choose the last option just because it's the most comfortable one. As Latinas, we're trained from an early age to put family first, and if we have to sacrifice our dreams, so what? It's our husbands and male children who are really important in this world, right? At least that's what the little voice in our heads says to us. But isn't that really *mamacita* we hear so clearly, telling us the right thing to do? It could be our mama, or grandmama, or even daddy we hear, but the sad part is that many Latinas not only hear that voice, they *listen* to it. I know because I did too. When I got married, I did the "proper" thing and left my father's house for my husband's house on my wedding day. And my husband's house was only a few blocks away, which made my *mamí* very happy!

Soon, though, I went through a divorce (the first in the family). I moved to Las Vegas. Even that was too much for my family, who begged me to return to the Fresno neighborhood of Orange Cove where I grew up, which I soon did. But by then I had learned that there was a world outside Fresno that I wanted to see more of and experience. None of my five brothers and two sisters have ever been farther away from Fresno than Mexico, while I've traveled the world over and even met the president of Mexico, Vicente Fox. So my first definition of success meant earning enough money—and building enough courage—to break away from my hometown, *mi pueblo*, and my parents.

> *It's truly a terrific time to be a Latina.*
>
> Maria Rivera-Albert, *president, National Hispana Leadership Institute*

In other words, you can build up your courage, if you need to, by constantly setting small goals that you can meet pretty easily. That way you'll be successful all the time, not just when you reach the top of the mountain. Don't set yourself up for disappointment by saying *I'll know I'm successful when*

1. I have a big house/car/boat/bank account *or*
2. I've earned the respect of the top person in my field *or*
3. I've gained the knowledge that I've changed the world

or whatever grand definition of success you've been dreaming about. Instead, let success be what you do every day. Say to yourself every morning, "I'll be successful today if. . . ." Then say, "I'll be successful this week if . . .," "this month if . . .," ". . . this year if. . . ."

> *You can build up your courage by constantly setting small goals you can meet pretty easily.*

The key to happiness, I think, is to make sure your actions move you in a forward direction, not one that simply feels good. A goal that might make you feel good is "I'll be successful today if I don't get fired," but that goal gets you nowhere because it's not leading you in a positive direction; instead, you will be staying in the same place. With such a goal you're only covering your head and trying to not look like a target when the boss is handing out pink slips. Even if layoffs are almost certain in your company, wouldn't you be a lot farther ahead if you said to yourself, "I'll be successful today if I learn a new skill"? Even if that skill is simply to have the courage to say "Good morning!" with confidence when the big boss walks by, it can really add up to something if you learn a new skill every day.

When you get to the end of your daily, weekly, monthly, and yearly successes, it's a certainty that you'll be a lot farther along in a positive direction than you are today.

Taking small steps in the right direction was my only goal when I was starting out, and that's exactly what I did. One day I saw a news story about a dentist moving into Orange Cove. I knew right away that if he didn't speak Spanish, he would need someone who did. I had no prior experience, no résumé. However, I spoke Spanish, and so I called him up and offered to do translation for his patients. That got me in the door. Then I noticed that he needed help getting his x-rays done, and so I learned how to do that. Eventually I learned enough about every job in the office to become his office manager. That was a good job, with a decent rate of pay, and all it took was looking around for opportunities to succeed at a higher level every day.

Of course, being open every day for opportunities to succeed means that you may move in totally unexpected directions too. That was how I got into TV. An old boyfriend of mine who owned a home-remodeling company wanted to air a commercial on the Spanish-language television station SIN to boost his business among Latinos. But when he was asked, "Who will be your talent?" (on-air spokesperson), he asked me. Whoa, I thought, not me. I used to be so afraid to get up and talk to anybody, and he wanted me to go on television? But then I thought, "What's the worst that can happen if I fail? They just won't show it. And who knows what this could lead to if I pull it off?" So I said to my boyfriend, "*¿Porqué no?*" "Why not?"

¿Porqué no? Why not?

WHY NOT? WHAT STANDS IN OUR WAY

When the day came to shoot the commercial, I was terrified and excited at the same time. I knew my lines, and when the cameras rolled, I did two perfect takes (the fact that I had had a vodka martini helped). That was the beginning of a career in television that has given me many more opportunities than I ever dreamed of as a migrant farm worker. None of those opportunities would have developed, though, if I hadn't had the courage to say, "*¿Porqué no?*"

Unfortunately, our culture gives us, as Latinas, plenty of reasons to be afraid of saying "Why not?" Many *Angla* women had the same problem until feminism came along to liberate them, but in many ways we Latinas missed out on the feminist movement and are still letting our society and culture keep us under its thumb. *Claro*, young Latinas will have an easier time than I did coming up, but pressures to conform in the Hispanic culture are still huge, no matter how long your family has been in this country. Why else would millions of families put themselves into debt for *quinceañera* parties they cannot afford, money that their 15-year-old daughters would be better off saving for college? And why else would Latinas continue to defer their dreams of personal success?

> *Pressures to conform in the Hispanic culture are still huge, no matter how long your family has been in this country.*

Don't misunderstand me. I'm not saying that Hispanic culture is something to be escaped, avoided, or looked down on. *¡Por favor!* Our culture is what gives us our spirit of celebration, our grace, our fierce determination. And heaven forbid that we should lose our sense of fun, our warmth, and our willingness to laugh at the crazy ways of the world. All those qualities, if we are not afraid to show them, give us strength and help us make a positive impression on people.

Nevertheless, Latinas face unique challenges that make succeeding—especially in the work world—doubly difficult. What do you do, *por ejemplo*, when you dream of conquering the world and *mami* cries because your dream will take you away from the old neighborhood? Can both of you be happy with your decision? Or can you at least find a way to live with each other's preferences? Yes, you can. *Sí, se puede.*

In my case, I suffered for years whenever I questioned my mother's wisdom. Every time I wanted to do something that would help me move in a positive direction, my *mami* always told me how hard it would be—on her! Especially when I wanted a career of my own, my family opposed it because they "knew" it would make my husband feel like less of a man. The black cloud over my head, and perhaps yours too, consisted of the dreaded words "What are people going to think?" "*¿El qué dirán?*"

What are people going to think? ¿El qué dirán?

Almost against our will, such attitudes become so ingrained in us that we don't even know they're holding us back.

Demographics:

- *There are over 35 million Latinos in the United States today, and nearly half are women.*
- *The Hispanic population is expected to grow to over 60 million by 2020.*
- *The future Latino population will have more second-generation Latinos (born in the United States of immigrant parents) than new immigrants from Latin countries.*
- *Fifteen percent of working Hispanics are college graduates.*
- *Latino purchasing power is more than half a trillion dollars annually.*
- *Over 1.5 million Latino households have incomes above $50,000 a year.*

Following are five major roadblocks—*cinco grandes obstáculos*—likely to stand in the way of Latinas as we try to rise above the crowd. The first step to overcoming them is to realize that they're only as powerful as you let them be.

Roadblock 1: Money Is Sinful

I've never had a bit of trouble accepting any money that came my way. But I've always had a little voice inside saying: "What makes you so good, Rico, that you deserve this?" It goes back to our Hispanic upbringing: Family and good times were always more important than having money. You don't need money, after all, to have a loving family, just as you don't need store-bought toys to have fun. For those of us raised Catholic, money is an even more guilt-ridden issue. The priests and nuns who were our spiritual leaders all took vows of poverty. What sinful people we must be to want more of it in our lives!

If you listen to that little voice, though, you'll always have trouble accepting money in your life. Worse, you won't look for opportunities to attract money toward you. To complicate matters, that little voice of poverty may not tell you directly to avoid a moneymaking opportunity. Instead, the voice will say things like, "Isn't that too risky?" or, "If it doesn't work out, do you really want to live in a box under a bridge?" Maybe the opportunity you're considering *is* too risky, but your voice of poverty will do everything it can to scare you off before you even consider all the angles. Some risks—in fact, many risks—turn out to be worth taking once you consider all the angles.

Think about this: I had to invest my life savings to become a partner in Entravision, the company that made me *rica* when it went public two years ago. Was it a risk to put up my life savings like that? Hell, yes. Was it an *unreasonable* risk? *¡Absolutamente no!* I understood from the start that I could lose all my money. But I carefully investigated my partners and knew we had a good idea. How could we fail when we wanted to reach a growing Hispanic market with as many media vehicles as possible? We certainly could have failed. We took a risk, a big risk. But once I was confident that there was more potential for gain than there was for loss, I jumped on it.

What does this have to do with your career? Everything. Every time you endure a terrible job because you think it will be too hard to get another one, you are refusing to take a risk. Every time you put up with discriminatory and sexist remarks at work without calling the offenders out, you are refusing to take a risk. Every time you put off taking steps to become the boss of a big company or of your own company, you are refusing to take a risk. You get the idea. Think of yourself as a female shark. A shark always has to move forward or it will die. Always move forward. Today's step might be a little one, but add up thousands of todays and you'll be way ahead when today becomes tomorrow.

Always move forward.

Roadblock 2: It's Impolite to Ask

I can't tell you how many employees I've had who could have moved ahead in their careers but didn't. Why? Because they were afraid to *ask* for what they wanted. For example, when I would question them about why they didn't apply for a posted opening that was perfect for them, they'd say they didn't think anyone wanted them for the job. In other words, they were waiting to be *invited* to apply.

This is a real cultural hang-up for us, and we learn it early. Didn't *mami* always tell you never to ask for anything at the neighbors' house? Don't ask for a cookie if you're hungry. Wait for Mrs. Jimenez to offer you one. Like Mrs. Jimenez was a mind reader? And never mind the neighbors. We weren't even supposed to ask *mami* and *papi* for anything beyond what they gave us. All this was supposed to help *todo el mundo* avoid embarrassment if they couldn't afford what you were asking for. I remember when my family went shopping for our first new vehicle. We wanted a white and blue Ford pickup. But the part I will never forget is when my dad looked at the sticker price in the showroom and flinched. I said: "Don't worry, Dad, that's not what you're going to pay. We'll negotiate a better price." And he said, "You can't ask for a better price. They'll think we can't afford it." *Mi papí* didn't understand that anything is negotiable if you ask.

Well, guess what? The company you are working for probably *can* afford to give you what you want and won't be embarrassed in the least if you ask. They can always say no—or yes. Ask.

Most companies, in fact, will make it a point to give you what you want if you prove you are valuable to them. Look around for extra jobs that need doing when you are finished doing your own job. Don't wait to be asked to take on the extra tasks: Volunteer! Try to improve your communication skills. Do you need to brush up on your grammar? Do it. Could you use a course in public speaking? I did that early in my career. Think about ways to do your job better and share them with your supervisor. Join organizations your superiors belong to and volunteer to help out on a visible project. Do anything, in fact, to get noticed in a positive way.

> *You have to choose what you want to do.*
>
> Salma Hayek, *actress*

Do anything to get noticed in a positive way.

Will doing all that get you a better job? Maybe. If you ask. Remember that you are selling yourself. Asking for the business is the key to making the sale. You also need to be prepared to haggle over the best price for your services. We Latinas are probably the world's best bargainers when it comes to buying things. But when it comes to pricing ourselves, helping set our own salaries, our instinct is to wait passively while someone tells us how much we're worth. I recently taught my niece some of my salary-bargaining tricks, and she negotiated a job offer thousands of dollars higher than the one the company originally offered her. Later in the book I'll tell you more about how you can do the same.

◆

Success means doing what you have to do even when you don't want to.

◆

Will asking for what you want be easy? Probably not, at least at first. But all successful women learn how to do it—because they have to. "Success means doing what you have to do even when you don't want to," says my friend Mary Ann Padilla, owner of the largest temporary employment agency in Denver. We'll hear more from her later, too.

Roadblock 3: Only Your Man's Comfort Es Importante

In the ideal Hispanic home, so we are told, any woman can have a career as long as she makes sure her husband's dinner is on the table and the house is spotless when he gets home. As long as our men are happy, the myth goes, we can do anything we want. But that's not really true, is it, *mujeres?* In reality, even if we do have the dinner on the table and keep the house spotless, that little voice in our heads tells us we're being bad girlfriends, wives, and mothers because we want something more. Heaven forbid that we should make a lot more money than our men do and be more successful in business.

The *macho* culture is alive and well in America, as much as we might wish it weren't.

And, like you, I've seen many Latinas let their men get away with outrageous things. Things that most *Anglas* wouldn't stand for anymore, many of us Latinas still accept without comment, even though we are boiling inside. Are you still the one stuck in the kitchen, preparing the feast during a *fiesta*, while the men sit outside telling jokes and enjoying beer and cigars?

Personally, I never accepted that this was the way things had to be. I was always outside hanging out with the boys. But I know that it's easier to ignore husbands who don't lift a finger around the house or colleagues who make disrespectful remarks at work than to raise a stink. We'll even settle for just having a job instead of pursuing a career for the sake of peace around the house. It's not really that bad, we tell ourselves, and *claro*, he's never going to change anyway. Don't you believe it! My daughters both have wonderful husbands, and boy, can they cook!

I felt intimidated by the men in my life for many years. I even let my husband hold me back for many years. He was a good man, a good husband, and a good father. What he did not have was the drive and passion that I felt was needed to take chances and grow. He was happy living in a small town, working from eight to five, but that was not what I wanted, which is why I didn't ask for child support or alimony or any property when I divorced him; I just wanted my daughters and a car and our clothes. *Oye no*, I'm not telling you that you have to be divorced to succeed in business. Far from it. You do have to take control, however. Speaking up about how things make you feel is the first step. You won't change your man overnight, but if he loves you, he'll eventually get the idea that your success and feeling of self-worth are important to his happiness too. (Exception: Once an abuser, always an abuser. You should get far away from those guys immediately.) I'll tell you more about how to help your husband or partner support your goals as we go along.

Speaking up about how things make you feel is the first step.

Roadblock 4: Successful Women Aren't Latina Enough

Sometimes people in your family or community may try to tell you that you'll be less of a Latina if you try to move ahead in the world. You'll have to become a *gringa* on the outside, they say, or prejudice will rear its ugly head and defeat you. The people who say these things are wrong even though their hearts are in the right place. They are trying to protect you from a world where discrimination is real. But you can't avoid prejudice. You'll encounter prejudice as a Latina no matter what you do, where you go, or how far you rise. If you pay attention to those attitudes, though, you'll be defeated before you start because you'll never try to make an impact as a Latina.

"The lack of Latina role models is a problem. If you don't see leaders who look like you, it's harder to model the most effective behaviors," says Marisa Rivera-Albert, president of the National Hispanic Leadership Institute. Marisa helps train hundreds of Latina leaders and teens each year and says that even the most successful ones struggle to find a way to blend their culture with the business world. Still, she says, we have unbeatable qualities when it comes to becoming leaders in our fields in spite of lingering prejudice: "Our Hispanic culture has taught us to be hard workers, ethical, loyal, and express pride about who we are. All are qualities of strong leaders."

> *Sixty percent of Latinos believe that it is still possible to start out poor in this country, work hard, and become rich.*

You can succeed in business and the world without losing your heritage by crafting an image that is all your own. Observe how powerful and successful women present themselves at your place of employment, in your community, on television, and in movies. How can you convey a similar image while retaining your own flair? Look around at successful women you meet or see on TV, *Anglas* and Latinas both. It should be obvious that you won't want to decide what to wear to work from what you see on the *telenovelas*. You'll notice that powerful women have a self-confidence, a pride, that seems to pour out from some secret place inside them. As we go along I'll let you in on the secrets of presenting yourself in a way that demands respect.

> *Powerful women have a self-confidence, a pride, that seems to pour out from some secret place inside them.*

How can you battle discrimination when it reaches up to slap you down? I encountered all sorts of prejudice when I was starting out in television. One of my first jobs was to sell ads on our Spanish-language station to local businessmen. After a few of them said, "We don't want any 'dirty Mexicans' shopping here," I did some research and found out how much money the Hispanic community spent on products like theirs. I can tell you, I changed a lot of minds when I decided to fight prejudice with facts.

If you can't change minds with facts—and prejudice is something that closes a lot of minds—do what Denver environmental engineering consultant Raydean Acevedo does: "My mom said to make a giant 'cancel stamp' in my mind and just bring it down hard on any hurtful words. Being able to shut out things you can't change is an awfully useful skill."

Only 15 percent of working Latinas have a college degree.

Roadblock 5: Latinas Don't Need an Education

To get ahead in the world, nothing beats a good education. Why start at the bottom the way I did? A person with a college degree can start many rungs up the ladder from the bottom and get ahead faster. If I had a college degree instead of a GED, I'm sure I'd be president of the United States by now! But we Latinas have the worst record of all Americans when it comes to finishing college: Only 15 percent of us have degrees. And that's not the worst thing: We are the least likely group to finish high school. Did you know that not finishing college cuts your total lifetime earning power almost in half?

Still, when your family discourages (or forbids!) you from continuing your education, they are not being cruel. They only want what's best for you. Unfortunately, many Hispanic families—especially immigrant families—don't have the same expansive view of life's possibilities that their daughters do. Just living in this country has given you the idea that anything is possible. But particularly for parents who were born in the "old country," what they've managed to accomplish here, even without much education, is often astounding to them: "Look how much better off we are than your cousins in Mexico!" It can be extremely difficult for them to understand why a daughter would want "more," particularly if she can't quite define what "more" is just yet.

> *Just living in this country has given you the idea that anything is possible.*

Besides, why encourage a girl to achieve when her husband will want to take care of her? He'll just feel threatened or useless, the reasoning goes, if his wife has more education or makes more money than he does. Maybe he will, but honey, you can't depend on a man anymore. According to the U.S. Census, in 2000 a full 20 percent of Latinas were divorced or widowed. *Créemelo*, I taught my daughters that there is no guarantee that your husband will be around, no matter what *papí* says. It's up to you to be able to take care of yourself no matter what happens.

The key to getting around this roadblock is to realize that your parents—or your husband, if he's standing in the way—probably want the best for you. You just differ on what "best" means. You have to become a teacher to your parents or your husband. Figure out why what you want to do is upsetting for them. Then think about its possible impact on your family. Figure out how to minimize that impact. Talk repeatedly about how your dreams will make the family stronger because you'll be stronger. And reassure them that the family will always be number one in your heart.

> *Your dreams will make the family stronger because you'll be stronger.*

And if that doesn't work? Everyone hopes for a supportive family, of course, but nothing says you can't go your own way without their permission. If you want to go to school but you can't afford it, find another way. Nelida Quintero, an *argentina*, worked with a librarian to find scholarship money specifically for Latinas when her parents had no money to send her to the art school her teachers told her she was qualified for. They told her no because they had to. She found a way past that to what she wanted to do with all her heart. She is now an architect with her own company in New York City. "Seize opportunities to advance," she says now. "You'll never regret pursuing your dream, even if it's very hard to do."

◆

SCHOLARSHIPS FOR LATINAS

An impressive number of organizations now offer scholarships for Latinas and other people of color. The list following is by no means the entire universe of such scholarships but includes many of the most generous. Latinas also can qualify for other, more generally distributed scholarships too, of course. For more information, see *Get Free Cash for College: Secrets for Winning Scholarships* by Gen and Kelly Tanabe (Los Altos, CA: Supercollege, LLC, 2003). You can also search for scholarships at fastweb.com.

- **American Meteorological Society Industry Minority Scholarships.** www.ametsoc.org

Applicants must be at least sophomores who are planning to pursue a career in selected sciences in which minorities are underrepresented.

- **American Society of Criminology Fellowships.**
  www.asc41.com/minorfel.htm
  Fellowships of $6,000 for three minority students annually in criminology or criminal justice.
- **FFA Minority Scholarships.**
  www.ffa.org/programs/schapp/index.html
  Scholarships of up to $10,000 for members of Future Farmers of America who are pursuing a college degree in agriculture.
- **Gates Millennium Scholar.**
  www.gmsp.org/main.cfm
  Funded by the Bill and Melinda Gates Foundation. For incoming freshmen in mathematics, science, engineering, education, and library science. Applicant must be a leader in extracurricular or community activities and be nominated by an educational official.
- **Hispanic College Fund Scholarship.**
  hispanicfund.org
  Open to any U.S. undergraduate interested in a career in business. Two hundred scholarships available each year of $500 to $5,000. Also has a program for students transferring from community colleges.
- **Hispanic Scholarship Fund.**
  www.hsf.net/scholarship
  Scholarships to encourage Hispanic high school and college students to complete a four-year university degree.

- **Jackie Robinson Scholarship.**
  www.jackierobinson.org
  Minority high school seniors who show exceptional academic achievement, leadership qualities, and significant financial need can qualify for these scholarships, which are named for the professional baseball player who broke the color barrier.

- **Legal Opportunity Scholarship Fund.**
  www.abanet.org/lje/losfpage.html
  First-year law students who demonstrate both financial need and community leadership can qualify for this $5,000 award designed to encourage minority representation in the legal profession.

- **LULAC National Education Service Centers.**
  www.lnesc.org/services.htm
  Scholarships are offered by the League of United Latin American Citizens (LULAC) through the organization's local councils.

- **Minority Dental Student Scholarship.**
  www.ada.org
  Up to $2,500 for minority dentists, to be based on financial need and academic achievement. Students must be entering the second year of dental school.

- **National Defense Science and Engineering Graduate Fellowships.** www.asee.org/ndseg
  A program for college graduates in science and engineering that allows them to reenter school and pursue a doctorate. Applications are particularly encouraged from women and minorities, with stipends of up to $21,000.

- **Radio & Television News Directors.**
  www.rtnda.org/asfa/scholarships/undergrad.shtml
  Famous broadcasters and journalists such as Ed Bradley and Carole Simpson have created scholarships to encourage minority students to enter the media. There are various qualifications for each one.

- **Raquel Marguez Frankel Scholarship Fund.**
  www.hermana.org/chpfrm.htm
  Awarded to outstanding Latinas based on academic excellence, leadership potential, and financial need. Sponsored by the MANA National Latina Organization, formerly the Mexican American National Association.

- **Rotary Ambassadorial Scholarships.**
  www.rotary.org/foundation/educational/amb_scho
  Study abroad for up to a year if you speak a foreign language fluently. Recipients must have completed two years of college.

- **Ruben Salazar Scholarship Fund.**
  www.nahj.org/student.html
  The National Association of Hispanic Journalists offers scholarships of up to $5,000 for Hispanic undergrads and grad students studying journalism.

- **Society of Hispanic Professional Engineers Scholarships.** www.shpefoundation.org
  Available to any student studying engineering or science. Each year, 250 scholarships of up to $7,000 are given.

BE A "LATINA TO THE MAX"

Yes, our culture has many ways to hold us back, but it can do that only if we let it. *La Vida Rica* is intended to be your road map over, around, and through the obstacles that will stand in your way. But you don't have to take my word for it. Many, many Latinas are now achieving levels of success they never dreamed of. You'll hear from some of these women, who have agreed to share the stories about how they made it. And you'll hear from ordinary women who are getting ahead every day because they refuse to accept what our culture tells us to be.

There's never been a better time to be a Latina.

And here's the best news of all: There's never been a better time to be a Latina. Corporate America has finally discovered that the Hispanic market is huge and is not assimilating into the U.S. melting pot. We're keeping our culture, *gracias*, and we're cool. Gloria Estefan, J-Lo, and Shakira make everyone want to shake it up. Dolores Kunda became president and chief executive officer of Lapiz Integrated Marketing when the giant Leo Burnett ad agency decided that it couldn't ignore the Hispanic market a *minuto* longer. "The U.S. is the world's second largest Spanish-speaking market. It was time for corporate America to wake up and smell the Cuban coffee!" declares Kunda, a *cubana* herself. Her company now does Hispanic advertising for Coke, Disney World, Kellogg's, and Sara Lee, among others. And she encourages Latinas to take advantage of their unique background: "The market is crying for well-educated Hispanics who are experts in their fields. This is the start of something big."

I agree completely. But you don't have to speak Spanish or work in something Hispanic-related to be a big success as a Latina. I'm here to tell you that you can be everything you want to be, and you don't have to sacrifice your family life to do it. I have two wonderful children and two wonderful grandkids that I love to death. I have all the professional satisfaction I could want. Even though I could afford to quit working today, I continue to work as the co-owner of a BMW dealership. And I'm still looking for opportunities to say, "Why not?"

You can get to the top of the mountain from here, too. I'll show you the way.

2
Finding Work That Makes You *Rica*

*H*ow can you find work that will make you rich? Well, I could give you a list of high-paying careers and say, "Go for it, *chica*. Pick a job that pays well, work hard at it, and spend your retirement years counting your cash." In fact, far too many ambitious Latinas choose a career in just this way. And *mira*, some Latinas are earning pots of money today because they picked careers they knew should lead directly to financial reward: They are lawyers, doctors, corporate executives, stockbrokers . . . and every other career that commands the big bucks. But more than a few of these high-powered ladies are miserable. Why? Because they hate the work they do.

I believe that achieving success in business is not all about making as much money as possible. Instead, living *la vida rica* means finding work that gives you professional and personal satisfaction. If you can manage that, you will attract más *dinero* automatically because you'll enjoy everything you need to do to advance your career.

> *Living* la vida rica *means finding work that gives you professional and personal satisfaction.*

Even better, if you can find something about the job you have that you love, you'll do your job better, which will open up hidden opportunities to get ahead. I spent many years selling advertising on Spanish-language TV, but I wasn't very good at it until I figured out how to make it my passion, *mi pasión*. That job became my passion when I realized that it was not only about selling advertising; it was also about helping my clients get more business. Because I am a Latina, it was natural for me to want to help other people find happiness. I finally realized that helping my clients do more business made them happy, and so selling advertising started to make me happy. Once I figured out that I was in the business of spreading happiness, my sales figures shot up like a rocket. I also found out that my steadily rising commissions made me very happy indeed. *Mi pasión* led me to become the best, most successful salesperson in Spanish TV.

> *Because I am a Latina, it was natural for me to want to help other people find happiness.*

Of course, your passion may not lie in sales. Many people would rather make a speech naked than try to sell anyone anything. My point is that you are doing yourself and your career a disservice if you don't try very hard to find your own *pasión*. Do you take pleasure in making numbers come out right? Do you like to write? Love to help people resolve their differences? Adore performing in public? Get a kick out of finding hid-

> *The more we learn to love ourselves, the more power we have to shape our own futures without being manipulated by others.*
>
> Yasmin Davidds-Garrido, *author of* Empowering Latinas

den bits of information? Love speaking *español?* Always want to be in charge and get things done? Whatever your passion is, your duty to yourself is to figure out what floats your boat.

Your duty is also to recognize that it's a bad thing to say "I have a passion about banking (or law or fashion designing) because I want to make a lot of money." No. What you are passionate about comes from inside and has nothing to do with a specific career or industry. In fact, for the rest of this chapter put aside any thoughts of a specific job, industry, or line of work. Your responsibility to yourself, if you want to live *la vida rica,* is to discover what makes your soul sing. Is your soul singing when you go to work each day? Or is it screaming, "Oh, *Madre de Dios,* not this again!"?

Discover what makes your soul sing.

Even if you do not hear actual screaming in your head, you may subconsciously be acting out your need to find your *pasión.* Do you find yourself procrastinating about projects? Are you late to meetings? Hardly ever inspired with new ways to do something? Hitting the snooze alarm every morning? Your *alma* is trying its best to get your attention. Are you listening? Please don't think that because you are relatively happy in your job or with your life, you have found your passion.

If you don't spring out of bed every morning bursting with ideas and eager to get to your job or your business, you haven't found *tu pasión.*

WHERE YOUR *PASIÓN* LIVES

Often we secretly know what our *pasión* is but are afraid to admit it to ourselves. It's something that gives us laugh-out-loud joy when we do it and probably has always come easily to us. Too bad it's so hard to honor our passions: "Oh, I'd never be able to make a living doing that, so why torture myself?" Or our parents urge us to be cautious: "*Mija*, be a teacher (or a banker or a lawyer). Then you'll always have a paycheck to fall back on." Therefore, we take a secure but not necessarily exciting job and then complain about how much we hate it. Why is that? Our parents and our subconscious fears want to protect us from the poverty and failure they are sure will follow our decision to follow our *corazónes*, our hearts. But I'm convinced that we need to follow the voice of our heart that's telling us what we love to do even if it seems that our passions are too unrealistic for words.

Our parents urge us to be cautious.

Maria Morales-Prieto, a *cubana* who is now the managing editor of *Latin Long Island* magazine, was a stay-at-home mom when she decided to follow her passion for writing. She was writing sitcoms that she still hopes to sell one day. But she decided she wanted a regular job as a writer, and so she wrote to the editor of a local magazine she loved, *Latin Long Island*, and told him about the kinds of articles she wanted to read: stories about real Hispanics and their triumphs. Her passion and good ideas for the magazine came through so clearly in her letter and a subsequent interview that the editor hired her almost immediately. "You can make your own wishes come true," she says. "That's especially true for Latinas right now. Companies are recognizing that there's a huge market out there for messages about our culture. And if you have language skills or even a cultural understanding of the Hispanic market, you are rare and valuable. You can name your price."

In other words, if you can find some way to combine your *pasión* with your Hispanic heritage, you'll be able to write your own ticket. Many of the Latinas we'll hear from in this book have done just that. But even if you don't capitalize on your heritage and it only adds spice to your work life, discovering your true *pasión* will add *muchos dólares* to your bank account—and to the *calidad* of your life. Trust me on this one.

Combine your pasión *with your Hispanic heritage.*

So, how does a person go about finding out where her passion lies? There are several ways to do it that have worked for me over the years. Yes, I said "over the years." Few people remain focused on a single grand passion for life. Most of us move from passion to passion as our interests change and our goals are met. Your passion today may not be—probably will not be—your passion 5, 10, or 20 years down the road. As you evolve personally and professionally, your passion probably will change too. Here are some ways to be always in touch with what makes your heart sing, *tu corazón canta*.

1. What's Difficult for Others Is Easy for You

We tend to devalue our greatest talents because they come so easily to us. Ambitious women want to be challenged by the work they do, and so if something is hard, they feel like they are headed in the right direction. But struggling to master something as opposed to learning new skills that fit you from the get-go are two vastly different efforts. My feeling is that if you are naturally good at something and it comes easily to you, your search for your passion should start right there. *¡Tu talento tiene valor!* Look within yourself for the talents you already possess and capitalize on them. My main talents have been Spanish-language fluency, confidence, and the ability to learn quickly. What comes most easily to you? Take a minute to jot those skills down somewhere. Call it your "Passion Cheat Sheet."

Look within yourself for the talents you already possess and capitalize on them.

Are your talents automatically your passions? No. That would be too easy, wouldn't it? You may have a talent for playing the piano but hate practicing. Piano playing is not your passion (at least not now) because of that element of hate. But you should look toward your talents for clues that may lead to your passions. When do you get joy practicing your talents? Can you identify what it is that is making you joyful? There's where your passion lies.

2. You Would Do It for Free

Even though I made a lot of money in my life, most of the time I would have done whatever job I had for nothing. I enjoyed my work that much. Of course, I would have had to find some way to feed my kids, but I feel privileged to have found work that has excited me, in television. You may know already what it is you would willingly do for free because you volunteer your time for a cause. When you commit yourself to volunteering and stick with it for a while, you eventually gravitate toward the tasks where your talents can be best used, toward your *pasión*. I do volunteer fund-

---

◆

You can succeed if you have persistence, performance, and mucho corazón.

Maria Rivera-Albert, *president, National Hispana Leadership Institute*

◆

raising for several nonprofit groups, including the Dumb Friends League, a shelter for animals, and the Mexican Cultural Center in Denver. I've discovered that my sales skills make me a great fund-raiser and that I get a real rush from persuading people to part with their money for donations. It puts a huge smile on my face to get donors to say yes. Whatever does that for you may be your *pasión*.

If you are unsure whether you'd do anything for free, think about when you were your happiest at work, even if it was only for a moment. Or maybe you're happy only when you're away from work (*pobrecita*). If nothing occurs to you right away, keep thinking. What were you doing when you felt your greatest happiness? Try to get more of that into your life, whatever it is. Perhaps you can volunteer for additional assignments at work that include that component or find a volunteer position that allows you to maximize your enjoyment.

Think about when you were your happiest at work, even if it was only for a moment.

Whatever way you find to do it, though, *do* it. When you are living your *pasión*, even a little bit, you'll be amazed at how eager influential people are to help you get more of it. When I was doing on-camera ads early in my career, I would have done that for free, no question. But the funny thing was, the station manager where we were filming literally begged me, over a period of months, to become a saleswoman there. Nah, I thought, I can't do that. The station manager saw, though, that I really enjoyed persuad-

> ◆
> *Success is measured in various ways. For me it is. Am I happy with what I'm doing?*
>
> Elena McEwan, M.D., *CARE, Inc.*
> ◆

ing people to buy things, and so he persisted. That was the beginning of all the good things that have happened to me.

3. Look Closely at the People You Admire

Who do you look up to? Is Jennifer Lopez your girl? Why? Because she can sing the *pantalones* off any guy? Or because she's a killer businesswoman in charge of a career that has gone from music to movies to fashion without end? Maybe you admire someone who is less well known. Is your most-admired person a hero of some kind? Or is that person someone you know really well? We are all drawn to certain people, whether they are celebrities, high achievers in our field, or members of our *familias*. The picture of your most admired person should be forming in your brain right now.

The people we admire most are the people we'd most like to be if we could. Another way to find your *pasión* is to figure out, *con exactitud*, what it is about these people that you admire. Write the person's name on your Passion Cheat Sheet and then list the qualities that made you single out that person. What really resonates for you? It's your *pasión* that's ringing that bell.

4. Threads from Your Past

Your subconscious mind may have been waving a red flag in your face for years, prodding you toward your *pasión*. Too often we Latinas ignore the signs that our desires throw out because they are not what we think we should do. Our *familias* tell us to get a good, safe job in an office. Or they tell us not to let a "good provider" get away because you're not getting any younger, are you, *chica*? But our subconscious desires come out loud and clear when we look at what we've been drawn to repeatedly, the threads that have repeated themselves from our pasts. One woman I know consistently took jobs where she was asked to work with numbers, but each time she'd find herself doing writing tasks for others in her workplaces "because she was so good at it." She eventually started her own writing business.

What we loved doing as *niñas* is often where our passion still lies. I found my *pasión* for negotiating business deals when I was 10 or 11 years old. That was when I started helping my parents deal with the English-speaking world. Other little kids might have resented being placed in a situation where they always had to speak for adults. I loved it. I was in the middle of negotiations (even though I didn't know to call them that) for everything *mis padres* wanted to buy, from cars to a house to dental services. I hadn't begun speaking English until first grade even though I was born in the United States. But once I became fluent in English, I loved being the go-between for my parents and helping them solve their problems. And that's been my *pasión* in everything I've done since. I've wanted to make money for my employers while making sure my clients were happy; I've wanted to make sure the deals I participated in left everyone satisfied; I've wanted my employees to find their own passions and always jump out of bed eager to come to work. It all comes down to understanding what makes me happy and striving to get more of that *salsa caliente* into my life. What did you love to do as an *hija?* Write it down.

What we loved doing as niñas *is often where our passion still lies.*

---

5. It's Part of Your Life Already

Your *pasión* doesn't have to be something you discover. It may just be something you realize you need to honor and capitalize on if you want to achieve business success. Is there something you're always talking about to the point where your *amigas* roll their eyes when you start in on it again? What do you have a lot of books about? What are you always writing about in your journal? (If you don't have a journal where you write down your hopes and dreams, start one today so that they can make themselves heard.) In other words, what surrounds you already that makes you excited?

Here's a great clue to *pasiónes* already in your life: If you always laugh when you're doing it, you may be on to something. An acquaintance of mine realized that she had surrounded herself with sailing books, boats, and talk of the open sea for many years, and so she decided she would not wait any longer to realize her dream to sail around the world. "If not now, when?" she asked herself. Unfortunately, she didn't have anyone who wanted to go with her. She advertised for an unmarried sailing partner who shared her passion and then married one of the guys who responded within three weeks (!) and headed off for her adventure. When she returned, she wrote and sold a book about her trip. Wasn't it dangerous to sail around the world with a total stranger? Well, I wouldn't have done it, but sailing is not my passion. My friend told me later that she recognized a corresponding fire for sailing in only one person among the many who answered her ad—and at the same time he recognized that fire in her. Marriages have been made on less, no? And how in the world did she afford the trip? Well, she got on the phone and raised the money herself. Passion can give you incredible energy when it comes to making things happen, especially when money is involved. A clear goal backed by *pasión* is an almost unstoppable force.

Passion can give you incredible energy when it comes to making things happen, especially when money is involved.

If all else fails and you just can't figure out what your *pasión* really is, I recommend that you find a way to go off by yourself. Take a short vacation by yourself in a rustic cabin with no TV or phones. Visit a convent for a week of retreat time. Or just send your family to a theme park for the afternoon, turn off the phone, and do nothing. (Or take the world's longest bath.) Start asking yourself questions: "What is it that I really enjoy doing?" "What should I be doing now?"

Ignore the little voice in your head when it shouts, "Find a TV!" and it will soon start delivering suggestions that could show you the way. Some of them may be incredibly impractical. Write them down anyway on your Passion Cheat Sheet (by now it's a notebook!) without censoring anything. Soon you'll have a wealth, as it were, of possibilities to explore.

Between 1990 and 1999 Hispanic women nearly doubled their employment in high-paying, highly skilled management and professional positions from 516,000 to 1,025,000.

HOW TO MARRY YOUR *PASIÓN* AND YOUR WORK

It's easy to make good decisions about how to spend your irreplaceable life if you can find out what you are passionate about. I was first struck by passion when I was sweating in the fields and trying to figure out how to get into the shade. But *pasión* jumps in whenever you feel strongly about anything. It's something you will sacrifice for: give up a *novio* for, lose sleep for, skip meals for, even give up your favorite *novela* for! Passion will motivate you to do what needs to be done for you to get what you want in life.

The problem arises when you've identified your passion and concluded—*ay caramba*—that your current job will never satisfy it. What do you do then? You find a way to move toward your passion, even if you can take only baby steps at first. For example, let's say you're looking through job listings on Monster.com. Some of the ads are bound to make you go "ewww," but others will have you saying, "Wow—in my dreams!" ("*¡Guau—mi sueño!*"). Reality rears its ugly head only when you read the "necessary experience" section. If you want to follow your passion, though, you'll want to print out every listing that rings your bell. Spread them out on the dining room table and write down what it is about each one specifically that makes the job seem attractive. When you have your list, figure out what the items on it have in common. *¡Claro, es tu pasión!*

> *Whatever job you take, be 100 percent responsible for getting it done. But don't look at it as just a job—have fun with it.*
>
> Mary Ann Padilla, *president and CEO, Sunny Side, Inc., employment agency*

Then there's the daring part: Apply for the jobs that turn you on the most even if you have no experience that "fits" the job description. Write a letter or make a phone call telling the person in charge exactly what turns you on about the job and exactly what you'll do to get up to speed right away. Unless you want to be a doctor, lawyer, engineer, or rocket scientist, most jobs—especially early in your career—don't require specialized training. (And if you really want to be a rocket scientist, what are you waiting for? You'll never be readier than you are now. As Ann Landers always said, "How old will you be in four years if you *don't* get that degree?)

> *And if you really want to be a rocket scientist, what are you waiting for?*

Offer to work for less money than the job would pay a fully qualified person or offer to work for free for a few weeks if you can afford to do that. Anything you can do to get into a job where your heart can sing every day at work will put you on the road to becoming *rica*, at least in spirit. Regla Perez Pino, a 35-year-old *puertorriqueña*, found her passion working at a temp job. Even though she had a college degree, she told the agency she'd take anything. One of her first assignments was as an administrator for MCI, the giant telecommunications company. Her job? Filling out expense reports. That wouldn't make my heart sing, but Regla found to her surprise that she loved finding new and better ways to make numbers jump through hoops. "I didn't even balance my checkbook before I took this job," she said, laughing. But what really turned her on was not the numbers but finding ways to do things more efficiently, and, not surprisingly, she soon was offered a full-time position. Not long after that, bored with number crunching, she applied for a job in MCI's corporate news bureau. As soon as she started, she took the initiative to create a database showing how MCI was being portrayed in both English-language and Spanish-language media.

"My bosses used what I learned to modify our messages about the company," says Regla. "I was very young with the company, but my work made an immediate impact." It must have. Regla has survived numerous layoffs at the troubled communications giant and is the corporate spokesperson for all issues related to Latin America. Pretty good for someone who started as a temp.

But that's just my point: You can start from anywhere and achieve a great deal of success if you concentrate on doing work that gets your motor running. That's the case because you'll be more motivated than the next *chica* to find a window when a door slams in your face. And you'll be more likely to recognize opportunities when they come along. Once you begin listening to your heart's desires, opportunities suddenly start wearing bright red hats. You can see them coming a mile away, and when they arrive, you're happy to invite them in for *café y pan dulce*.

> *You'll be more motivated than the next* chica *to find a window when a door slams in your face.*

Unfortunately, even when you recognize one of those big red hats, you still may be tempted to stay in your safe, familiar rut. After I had been working at the TV station in my hometown of Fresno, California, for several months, a friend told me about a great job at a station in Providence, Rhode Island. I would be the local sales manager, involving a big promotion and salary raise for me. But it would be at an English-language station and, worse, would be clear on the other side of the country from my *familia*. I'd always lived near my family. My kids were still in high school, too. And worst of all, it was Rhode Island. (Didn't they have snow in July there?) I did know they would not be serving piña coladas.

Still, I knew it was a promotion: I would be moving ahead and would be able to sell on a grand scale to the movers and shakers of the world. I recognized that I was faced with an opportunity and only had to overcome the negative brain chatter that all Latinas face when they try to break out of their comfort zones.

BRAIN CHATTER THAT LATINAS (ESPECIALLY) MUST OVERCOME

That little voice in our heads is something we can never turn off completely, but we can learn to control it. You know that voice: It's the one that tells you you'll never be smart enough, pretty enough, or *whatever* enough to succeed. Psychologists believe we're hearing the voice of whichever parent was the hardest to please. Some call it "the Internal Critic." And, like that parent, all the Critic is trying to do, really, is protect us. It wants us to shy away from growing because that might cause us pain. It wants us to walk the straight and narrow path because then we won't make mistakes. Most of all, it wants us to honor our family's way of doing things even when that way hasn't done anyone much good. Here are some of the things your Critic may be chattering in your ear.

Psychologists believe we're hearing the voice of whichever parent was the hardest to please.

Chatter #1: Small Is Safe

Our *familias* tell us to get a job with a steady paycheck and stick with it no matter what. Especially if they were immigrants to this country, such thinking makes sense—to them. A safe, secure job paying enough money to feed the children was enough, at least for my parents. But even when I was very little, I saw that people all around us had bigger homes and better cars than we did. Their kids had more than the three homemade dresses I had to wear to school, more than one pair of shoes that they needed to take off right after school so that they would last. And eventually I saw that my parents had worked all their lives and ended up with a big *nada*. *No, es verdad,* thinking small is *not* safe if you ever hope to be successful in life.

Chatter #2: Other People Will Resent Me

Are you keeping a lid on your ambition so that your *amigas* won't think your head is getting all swelled up? (*¿Se te sube a la cabeza?*) Are you afraid of earning more money than your *marido* does? Of not being able to get home by 6 p.m. to make dinner for everyone? Certainly not, you may be saying to yourself right now. But have you gotten over it? Fear of "what other people think" (*¿el qué dirán?*) was what kept our mothers in their places, and they tried their best to pass on the family's way of doing things to us. Whether we bought it consciously or not, something inside us internalized those messages.

Remember, it's that internal voice we're talking about now. Listen closely when you're thinking about career moves and you may be surprised at how much importance your Internal Critic attaches to other people's opinions.

Chatter #3: I'm Not Good Enough

This is the real killer. How can you make anything of yourself, your Critic wonders, when you're so obviously inferior to everyone else? Better to play it safe and not tell the world that you are in over your head already, it counsels. This chatter is especially powerful, of course, because it can point to chapter and verse of all your previous "failures" in life: that test you tanked in high school, the day you forgot about an important business meeting, that "surefire" deal you were going to close that didn't. Sure enough, all your mistakes will get trotted out by your Critic as soon as you try to move forward in any way. "See? You couldn't do it then, and you can't do it now." It matters not a bit that you have learned a great deal from each and every mistake you've made. Your Critic is determined to make sure you never make another one.

Chances are, your critic has been whispering these *palabras* and many more nasty little morale breakers in your ear for years. The idea is to make you too fearful to try to break out of your rut and go for the glory. Your Critic figures that if you're scared, you won't try, and if you don't try, you won't fail. Reality check: If you don't try, you'll never get anywhere. You've got to get that sucker off your back.

And here's how: Have a talk with your Critic. I'm serious! The next time you find yourself delaying or dithering about something, take out a piece of paper and write down: "Okay, Critic, why don't you think I should do this?" You'll be amazed to find that an answer of some kind will pop into your mind almost immediately. Don't censor it; write it down. Keep writing even if the only thing you can think to write is, "This is silly." Keep asking your critic questions and eventually you'll discover the hidden fears that are holding you back. And once you know what they are, you can deal with them consciously.

If you subconsciously fear that you don't have enough training to achieve your dreams, go get some. If you fear that you'll be neglecting your family if you reach for your goals, talk to them and work it out. If you fear you're just not talented enough, trust me, a lot of people got where they are in life with less talent than you have in your little finger. It's mostly a matter of acting confident until you feel confident.

If you fear that you'll be neglecting your family if you reach for your goals, talk to them and work it out.

My thinking throughout my career whenever I tried something new was that I could always go back to what I was doing before. Therefore, I was always trying to stretch a bit and see if I could travel just a little bit farther down the road toward achieving personal and financial success. Your family is going to tell you that you're crazy to give up a sure thing. In fact, they may do everything they can to get your Critic screeching in unison with them. My niece Angelica recently thanked me for encouraging her to take a six-month vacation in Spain when everyone else in the *familia* was saying, "*¿Estás loca?*" My own sister (her mother) was upset for days. But I knew I had to tell Angelica the truth: If you refuse to follow your heart, you're always going to wonder, "What if?" Regretting what might have been is infinitely worse than making an honest mistake. Besides, like my niece, you could find that pursuing your dream is the best decision you ever made.

If you refuse to follow your heart, you're always going to wonder, "What if?"

TAKE "THE PLEDGE"

I recently heard something that made a lot of sense to me: When you want to bring something new into your life, you need to pledge consciously that you will leave something else behind. I did just that early in my career when I took a big pay cut to get started in television, although I didn't put that name to it. You may be thinking, "Yeah, right. What's so *difícil* about that? I'd work in TV for free!" but you have to realize that I was a single mom with little kids at home. We needed every penny of the paycheck I was getting every two weeks, and here I was proposing to bring in a third, less steady income every month with only the *hope* that I'd earn enough in sales commissions to keep us afloat. To overcome the anxiety I felt about what I was about to do, I had to promise myself that I'd do everything in my power to make sure my kids wouldn't suffer from my ambition. In other words, I'd sell my ass off. However, what that turned out to mean was that before I started to earn a good commission, I had to work three jobs. I sold advertising during the day, did a talk show once a week, and then was a retail clerk at night. Pretty soon I wanted to give up, to do anything but sell. But whenever I go into something, I always find a way to make it work. And finally, after about a year, I began to earn more than I had at my previous "steady job."

But I might not have made myself so crazy—might have even learned to sell more quickly—if I'd heard about the power of "the Pledge." I might have looked harder for ways to live on less income, for instance. Could my daughters and I have moved in with a relative? Could I have asked for a loan from a friend or a bank? Should I have asked for child support? I'm sure that if I had concentrated every atom of my being on selling, I could have succeeded long before I did.

So listen to me when I tell you: Once you decide what your dream, your passion, is, you must also take the Pledge to leave behind the one thing that is holding you back the most. You might decide that what you need most is to move to a new city, leaving behind friends and family, and declare your independence. If that's what you need to do, pledge to do it before you do anything else. Otherwise you'll just dither and hesitate, succeeding only in getting in your own way. Or you may need to give up that job by a set date, say, six months from now, so that you can pursue your dream. Then do it whether you have something else lined up or not! The world has a way of opening doors when a passionate person makes a real commitment to a course of action, and that's what you do when you pledge to do seemingly irrational things such as leaving a steady job without having a new one waiting. You demonstrate to the person who most needs convincing—you!—that you are truly serious about what you've set out to do.

> *You must take the Pledge to leave behind the one thing that is holding you back the most.*

Caroline Pineras, a *colombiana* and president of Bilingual Staffing Solutions in Atlanta, has been serious about succeeding since she began working at age 14. By the time she was in college, she was going to school by day and working by night. Studying would start at 11 p.m.. Sleep? Who had time? But she persevered, got her degree, and eventually started her own business to match Hispanic candidates with jobs that capitalize on their unique skills. "Companies are starting to recognize that there is a huge need for people who understand both English and Hispanic cultures and languages," she says. "But people who really want to succeed—to work where their hearts lie—have to focus on their passion completely. If you just take any job, your heart will keep looking. You must have something that you love getting up in the morning to do. You must have that fulfillment in order to have a happy life. I do."

Yes, it's that simple. Identifying your passion and then fighting with all your strength and cunning to achieve it is really that powerful. Does finding your *pasión* guarantee that you will earn millions as I have? No, of course not. Some people find that their hearts lie in nurturing others or teaching, notoriously low-paid callings. Yet even those skills can be applied in a corporate setting (training, managing) if one of your dreams is also to make a generous amount of money.

In fact, six-figure incomes are becoming increasingly common for talented, ambitious women. According to the U.S. Department of Labor, almost 20 percent of those who make more than $100,000 a year in America are women. That percentage should be higher, of course, but it shows that the dream is hardly impossible. Twenty percent means that right now *millions* of women are earning six figures or more! And you can be one of them. Barbara Stanny, who talked to more than a hundred of these substantial earners for her book *The Secrets of Six-Figure Women*, learned that they all did one thing that seemed to set them on the road to *la vida rica:* They decided to pursue their passion. "The six-figure women I interviewed," she writes, "often spoke more animatedly about their private awakening than their financial advancement, about discovering the essence of who they are, the meaning and purpose of their lives, and expanding the boundaries that had limited not only their livelihood, but their entire existence as well."

In other words, money, sometimes pots of it, should be seen as gravy, *aderezo*. In my opinion, the real definition of success is not "Can I buy everything I see?" but "Am I giving the best of myself every day?" Those who can answer *sí* to the second question are the women who are truly *ricas*. The good news is that if you are doing what God intended you to do, the money usually will follow. It almost can't help itself. Financial reward tends to seek out those who use their talents to the fullest, as long as they make sure the world hears about what they're doing. (More about that in Chapter 4.) If the money doesn't

---

You must have something that you love getting up in the morning to do.

Caroline Pineras, *president, Bilingual Staffing Solutions*

---

come, though, people who have found their *pasión* don't really mind when all is said and done. They're ecstatic with their lives and their work anyway.

That's not to say that you shouldn't strive to get as much of the *dinero* as you can. For us Latinas especially, it's our turn. And the best way to put yourself in the way of big money is to take charge of your destiny by taking full control of your work life. You can do this by starting a business, investing in emerging businesses, or simply becoming president of your own career. The dream, *el sueño*, of success is already in your mind. Are you ready to live it?

3
Be the *Presidente* of Your Own Life

Let's be honest: Being the boss is better than being bossed. You set the hours and make the decisions, including how much to pay yourself. And you get all the glory when things go well. There's nothing to equal the high you get when an enterprise you are in charge of succeeds. Surprisingly, even when things go badly, it can be a lot of fun to be in charge because it is in your power to be the heroine if you save the situation. But here's an even bigger surprise: You don't have to be a manager or business owner to take charge of your life. *Sí*, you can get the glory even though you aren't yet *la jefa*.

The key is learning how to be the best boss you ever had—to become the owner of your own life. In other words, instead of looking upward for motivation and inspiration, you look into yourself. Looking inward is almost certainly going to get you a better quality of supervision, anyway. Who cares the most about you and your success, after all? You do, and so it's only fair that the person who is in charge of your success be you.

"Being my own boss" has been the longed-for goal of many of my Latina friends and coworkers over the years. However, not very many of them realized that their goal was within their reach all along. You don't have to start your own business to be the boss, although you certainly can if that's what you really want to do. You can be your own boss even if you are on the bottom rung of your company's ladder to the top. How? By being the CEO of your career.

You can tell when *mujeres* have taken ownership of their work lives. Even if they are only bank tellers or retail clerks, there's a confidence in the way they move. They walk firmly but with ease and flair, as well as great posture. They look you in the eye when you speak and always listen to what you have to say. They have a firm handshake and offer it to everyone, even to other women. When they speak, their voices are calm and controlled and you can hear every word distinctly even if those words have an accent. (These confident, in-charge women consider accents to be simply a unique aspect of their personalities.) Their words mean something too: Everyone in the company eventually learns that these self-controlled women can be depended on to do whatever they say they will do. In fact, they do more than what's expected of them, *sin preguntarles*.

> *Their voices are calm and controlled, and you can hear every word distinctly, even if those words have an accent.*

Let me explain the last point. You see, women who are in charge of themselves and their own careers don't really need to be supervised. They know the requirements of the job through training or observation, and they do those things as a matter of course. Then, without being asked, they look for other jobs that need doing, and they do them without necessarily looking for a promotion or *el dinero suplementario*. They look for ways to improve the company's operation even in the smallest ways. They make suggestions about big improvements too, even though they know they are unlikely to be able to implement those changes until they move up in the company. Going above and beyond the call of duty simply is a way of life for these women.

Are they nuts? Crazy like a fox, more like it. Do more than you're asked and you will be noticed. Give your best effort on a project that is important to *el jefe* and you'll be short-listed for promotion. Do whatever you can to solve problems instead of whining about them and you will be singled out as a rising star.

That's what happened to Kathleen Martinez, a 31-year-old single mom who now is a multicultural marketing manager for Southwest Airlines. When she joined the company in 2001, its effort to attract travelers from the Hispanic community was splintered and less effective than it could have been. By going out of her way to develop relationships with influential groups such as the U.S. Hispanic Chamber of Commerce and the Hispanic Heritage Awards Foundation, she has made Southwest a more vocal presence in the community. She also launched the Soaring Scholars program, a partnership with the Hispanic Scholarship Fund and *Latina* magazine, which will introduce Southwest to a whole new generation of budding businesswomen. The result? She was promoted to her current position less than a year after joining the company.

Kathy isn't a pampered rich woman with all the advantages, either. She grew up as the youngest of fourteen kids. Her parents didn't want her to go beyond community college, but she graduated from a good four-year school, eventually working as a congressional press secretary and founding an international trade fair in Laredo, Texas. She simply wanted to do everything she could to make the most of herself, including taking charge of her career. "You must take ownership of your work and look beyond your job description," Kathy advises other women looking to follow in her footsteps. "Don't ask 'Why do I have to do this?' but 'Why is the company doing this?' Find something to truly care about and then figure out how you can make even the smallest difference."

You don't even have to toot your own horn—much. In fact, you should be careful not to brag about any of your efforts to get ahead, at least at work. Nothing brings out the backstabbers like someone who is trying to "be better than us." However, a casual comment occasionally when you meet a higher-up is not out of line: "I really enjoyed creating that new system to track Latin American sales figures. I hope I'll be able to work on something similar for you again soon." As long as it sounds natural and not like sucking up, such brief comments help ensure that your accomplishments will be known in the right places and that you will get credit when it's due.

HOW TO BECOME THE CEO OF YOUR OWN LIFE

Right now, today, you too can change your mental attitude toward your life and career and become the best boss you ever had. Once you start viewing yourself as the CEO of your life, you'll be amazed at what you can accomplish. For one thing, it will become apparent to you quickly that the sky's the limit. Whatever you can imagine, you can try. You can go after the maximum amount of money; alternatively, you can satisfy your inner artist, which may pay little or nothing. Or you could fashion any unique career that satisfies you. Nobody says no to the CEO, remember.

Being the CEO of your life also means paying attention to a wide variety of essential functions. As the CEO of your career and your life, you are both the employee and the business owner, both labor and management, both the orchestra and the conductor.

Doing your current job to the best of your ability, in other words, is not the only thing you have to do to succeed. Rather, the successful woman needs to wear a sometimes astonishing variety of hats to pull off a career. But don't let this worry you. Much of the fun in a great career comes from the sense of being completely in control of one's destiny. That includes deciding which hat fits best on any given day, in any given hour, at any given moment.

> *If I had known it was such fun to have my own business, I would have started one right away.*
>
> Grace Williams, *president, National Association of Hispanic MBAs*

Hat #1: Steady Production

There's no way around it: You must work in order to get paid. But many ambitious people kick it up a notch further: They set production goals, promising themselves to spend X amount of time at the computer each day, produce X number of tangible results per week, and churn out a certain quantity of production, whatever that means in their particular jobs. I think these are all excellent ideas. Whenever I set production goals, I find that my productivity soars along with my sense of empowerment. Do I always set and meet goals? Unfortunately, no. And I don't beat myself up when I fail. But having specific goals helps, trust me.

A good way to force yourself to set and meet goals is to recruit a "work-it partner" (*"compañero de trabajo"*). Each week you and your partner promise each other to accomplish a set of tasks, both weekly and long-term. If you do, you get whatever reward you've promised yourselves (a massage? a party?). Your partner should not only monitor your progress but also give you feedback on whether you are trying to accomplish too much (or not enough) and whether you are staying on track toward your dreams. At the end of each week, not only do you get the promised reward if you meet your short-term goals, you get praise from your partner.

Your partner should be someone at approximately the same place you are in your career and with a similar degree of hope for success. You don't have to be in the same industry or working on the same kinds of projects. Your partner doesn't even have to live in your part of the world as long as she (or he) understands where you want to go in life. Most of us have at least one friend or acquaintance like that, and that person is likely to be flattered when you ask her or him to "work it" with you.

Hat #2: Meticulous Quality Control

Getting a lot done, though, is not enough. Because you're a *mujer*, your work has to be that much better than the work of *los hombres*. Yes, of course, this double standard should be a thing of the past. Reality check: It isn't. Women still can't afford to be associated with work that is anything less than excellent. That means making that last research phone call you'd rather not make. It means meeting or beating deadlines, always. It means double- and triple-checking facts and calculation methods. It means doing everything in your power to avoid making a mistake.

> *Your work has to be that much better than the work of* los hombres.

At the same time, you can't become so obsessive about details that you lose sight of the big picture. Always try to offer a new approach to the problem or project you're working on. Sure, the majority of the time the response to your creative ideas will be something like, "We just don't do things that way around here." Even if you hear that 9 times out of 10, don't stop offering ideas. And if your idea gets "stolen" by a higher-up, don't give up. You are trying to establish a reputation for beyond-the-call thinking. Don't whine if your ideas are not accepted, but if you fail to get credit after a few ideas *are* accepted, start looking for a new boss. Remember above all that your aim as "CEO of you" is simply to promote yourself as the "go-to girl" when clever ideas are needed. Don't sweat getting credit in the meantime.

- *There are an estimated 470,344 privately held firms owned by women in the United States, employing nearly 198,000 people and generating over $29 billion in sales.*

- *Between 1997 and 2002, the number of Latina-owned firms increased 39 percent and sales grew 8 percent.*

- *Nearly 4 in 10 firms owned by minority women are owned by Latinas.*

- *Firms owned by Latinas now represent 8 percent of all privately held, women-owned firms in the United States.*

- *Latinas start businesses at three times the national rate and are the fastest-growing segment of the small business community.*

- *Nearly one-third of all Latino-owned businesses are owned by women, employing 12 percent of the workers and accounting for 11 percent of the sales of Latino-owned firms.*
- *Some 55 percent of Latina-owned firms are in the service sector, 12 percent are in retail trade, and 5 percent are in consumer goods.*

Still, doesn't all that research, creativity, and deadline beating take a lot of time? Doesn't *la familia* at home deserve your attention too? *Sí* to both questions. The solution? If you don't want to be overwhelmed during your drive for success, you must learn to say no.

Latinas—myself included—find it very hard to say no in any circumstances. Most of us were brought up in nurturing, loving environments where the word *no* was the height of rudeness. *Mi papi*, a very poor man, could never refuse any request, especially for cash. "They need it more, *m'iya*," he'd say. And he was right; the people who came to him for help were always worse off than we were. To maintain a high level of quality, though, it is important to choose your battles. Always consider how any request pertains to your goals. *Most importantly*, always be prepared to give something up for every new responsibility you take on. (Remember "the Pledge" from Chapter 2?)

> *It took me time to learn that I had to say no to a lot of things.*
> Penelope Cruz, *actress*

Latinas—myself included—find it very hard to say no in any circumstances.

Hat #3: Forward-Looking Marketing

As the CEO of your life, you should always be looking for opportunities to meet the needs of your customers. Who are your customers? They are not who you might think. They are not your employer's customers. *Your* customers are the people who may be able to influence your career either in the short term or years from now. After all, you don't want to waste time marketing yourself to people who can't help you get where you want to go.

But beyond making yourself known, you want those important people to respond to your efforts to market yourself. To do that, you must focus on how your passions intersect with *their needs*. Marketers call this consultative selling. That is, instead of telling people what *you* want, you find out what your customers want to buy. For example, in the consultative selling model you'd never send people your résumé (unless asked) with the idea of interesting them in you. Why? Because your résumé is about you, *not* about your customers' needs. Instead, you'd figure out what you could do for the people you want to notice you. Can you introduce them to someone they should meet? Send them some information that they'll find useful? Point them toward a potential customer? Invite them to a *fiesta*? Whatever you do doesn't have to be elaborate or costly. It simply has to reflect thought—that you've thought about what your contact might be interested in. Focusing on their needs rather than your own, even for a few minutes, will give you clues about what you can do to help your best "customers." More often than not people remember and reward someone who has done a memorable service for them. Think about someone right now who could help your career. What could you do for that person today that would demonstrate that you were thinking about his or her needs?

Hat #4: Constant Publicity

If a tree falls in the forest, does anyone hear it? If no one knows about the good work you do, have you really done it? Yes, you have, darn it. *¡Claro que sí!* The problem is letting people know about it without seeming annoyingly self-serving. As I mentioned above, you only need to be alert for opportunities to mention your work as a positive example that is relevant to a topic under discussion. There are four caveats here, though: (1) It must be truly relevant, (2) it can only be said in passing, not dwelled on, (3) the same example shouldn't be used more than once with the same person, and (4) you can't do it very often. How often is too often? If you are bringing up your contributions daily, it's probably too much; once a month, probably too little. Quick hits almost below the level of conscious awareness are what you should be striving for: a sentence or two, no more. Otherwise you'll be seen as bragging, currying favor with the boss, or self-serving in the extreme. Leave people wanting to know more about you, not begging to know less.

When possible, you also should try to spread the publicity around. Like a good CEO, you can create a positive, supportive atmosphere around yourself just by making sure your coworkers are seen in the most positive light. Citing the good work of others as often as possible is an excellent way to encourage them subconsciously to do the same thing for you. When praise for you comes from someone other than yourself, it has a powerful effect on those who hear it. It's like the difference between an advertisement and a news story. The news story may have arisen from a press release, but it is more believable than the advertisement simply because it isn't directly self-serving. The same positive effect will come from praise for your work that doesn't come directly from you.

Hat #5: Humane Human Resources

As the CEO of your career, you are also in charge of keeping your production staff (that is, you) happy. Too many ambitious women focus on their production and marketing goals to the detriment of their physical, mental, and marital health. Working is, let's be honest, stressful. You're trying to sell yourself and your abilities, holding yourself to high standards, and producing at top speed, all the while taking care of your family—and carrying it off *con estilo*. But if you're not making time to exercise, eat and sleep right, and, *sí*, even take vacations, you're not going to be much good to anyone for very long.

Too many women give up exercise, eating right. and, especially, sleep in order to get ahead. For years I got by on as little sleep as I could because I felt I always needed to be working and striving to get ahead. Does that mean that you have to give up sleeping in order to be successful? *¡Absolutamente no!* In fact, I now believe I could have been even more successful if I had gotten more sleep every night. Women who boast about getting by on tiny amounts of sleep each night (six hours or less) don't realize that they could get more done and cope with problems better if they got the rest they needed. How do you know if you need more sleep? Sleep researchers have found that sleep-deprived people sitting in a dim room with nothing to do will fall asleep in about five minutes. Well-rested people will not crash no matter how long they sit there.

I have a theory about why we deprive ourselves of sleep to this extent. Ambitious women are so focused on winning at work that they can't shut it off at night. I slept much better once I started keeping a pad beside my bed to write down my worries before going to bed. Sometimes I'd even call my voice mail to record my ideas if worries woke me up. I could rest only when I got all those work thoughts out of my brain each night.

Sleep researchers have a theory about why we short ourselves on sleep. "I believe some people actually prefer being sleepy," says Timothy Roehrs, Ph.D., director of research at the Sleep Disorders Research Center at Henry Ford Hospital in Detroit. "It takes the edge off life, like a tranquilizer. All the events of life are then a little bit less sharp and more easily tolerated." Unfortunately, to make progress we need to have that edge, be light on our feet, *siempre*. And you can't do that when you're yawning over your third cup of *café*.

It should go without saying too that you need the energy that good food, exercise, and vacations provide. Don't live on tacos or you will be . . . *gordita*. If you exercise vigorously every day, you can pretty much eat what you want. Even an occasional doughnut or brownie won't kill you, as long as you eat a balanced diet that is rich in protein. That's what will give you energy for the long haul.

Finally, your personal "human resources" department should allow you at least two weeks of complete vacation every year, longer if possible. Notice that I said *complete* vacation. Leave your laptop and pager at home. Emphasize the fact that your cell phone number is to be used for emergencies only or go somewhere where you can't get a signal. The office can do without anyone for two weeks, especially if you develop plans for your subordinates to follow if something goes wrong. In fact, they'll probably be happy that you're out of touch. It will give them a bit of time to stretch their own wings. (Encourage them to make their own decisions while you are gone; that will make them better employees.) While you're at it, stretch your own wings. Don't just lie on the beach and veg out. Visit your ancestral home, *tus raíces*, to explore your roots. Volunteer at an archeological dig. Go skydiving. Do anything that will free your mind. You'll return home refreshed and recharged.

Hat #6: The Big Enchilada

Your final hat says you're in charge of what happens to your life. You're the top dog, starting today. No more drifting along where the winds blow you, following someone else's orders, taking the easy way out. Putting on this hat is like saying, "I'm in charge now, world. Look out," and then acting the part.

As the CEO of your life, you're the one who will make your "production department" snap to attention, who will direct your personal marketing campaign, who will decide how the employee (you) is going to be treated. You also will negotiate every little and big deal you have in the world, always making sure you are moving toward your dreams. Most important of all, if you want your *vida* to become *rica*, you will decide consciously when to play it safe and when to take big risks. Taking risks isn't all that scary if you know the right way to do it.

FIERCE AND FEARLESS: THE RIGHT WAY TO TAKE RISKS

Latinas in all walks of life learn to avoid taking risks early in life. We are encouraged to depend on our fathers, brothers, and husbands to make the right decisions. Under the protection of *un hombre*, we can be made safe from harm and never have to worry about a thing. At least that's the theory. *A veces*, we learned from watching our mothers cope with adversity that great reserves of strength reside in Latinas. If only we can learn how to tap into it, great things can be ours. We can be lionesses—*leonas*—if we can just have faith that things will turn out right when we take a chance. Sure, we'll fail sometimes. The key is to learn from failure, change gears, and not be afraid to take another risk.

Great reserves of strength reside in Latinas.

I took a big risk when I got involved with those two guys who later became my partners in Entravision and helped me make millions. They called me out of the blue one day when I was working at the TV station in Fresno. They were a couple of *hombres* who thought that Spanish-language media was going to be *caliente* (hot, hot, hot) in the future, and they wanted to build a company that would own Hispanic media nationwide. The starting point would be acquiring a radio license that was up for grabs in Madiera, California. To make their application more attractive, they needed someone Hispanic in the television industry to invest. Would I be willing to put up some money to become a partner? The trouble was that they could not tell me how much I would have to invest.

I was intrigued but extremely hesitant, as you can imagine. I had only a little bit of savings and young daughters to raise, and I didn't know these guys from Adam. Still, I knew from my experience in the industry that they were "on the money" about the potential of Spanish-language media. I decided that if I could minimize my risk, I'd take the leap. I approached my dealings with them as if it were a sales negotiation and tried to fashion the most favorable deal for myself. We ended up agreeing that I would owe nothing if we didn't get the license and only a couple of thousand if we did. It does not sound like a lot of money in hindsight, but it was almost all the money I had in the world then.

Once we had it in writing (approved by a lawyer), I rolled the dice and became their partner. We did get the license and I did give them the money, all without ever meeting them in person. Crazy? Probably. But you can't argue with how it turned out. Entravision is now a $1 billion public company that just bought another television station for $200 million. My partners tried to buy me out for $1 million a few years ago, right before the company was set to go public. Wow, I thought, a million in cash just to walk away. But I ultimately decided to take one last risk and participate in the public offering. It could have made me rich—or it could have failed and left me with a lot of worthless shares. Guess what I did? Right. I turned down the million that was being handed to me and ended up with a lot more green!

> *It bears repeating that there's probably never been a better time to be a Latina in this country, so ride the wave.*
>
> Sylvia Martinez, *editor in chief,* Latina *magazine*

Are you going to be asked to invest in that kind of thing out of the blue? Probably not. Are you going to be confronted with risks that could pay off handsomely in the end? Undoubtedly so. Are you going to be ready to risk whatever it takes? You will if you want to be *adinerada* (moneyed).

Let's say you are confronted with an opportunity or have an idea that might make you a lot of money. Here is a way to evaluate whether it is worth it to take a risk.

Can You Afford It?

Think about the worst possible outcome if you take this risk. Assume that everything will go wrong. How much would that terrible outcome cost you in money, time, and missed opportunities? Could you live with that? In contrast, suppose everything went right and your venture was a big success. Would you have enough money or time to cope with something that was growing by leaps and bounds? This often happens to people who open small businesses. Although they hope to succeed, they believe their operation will stay small and manageable for some time. If instead it takes off like a rocket, they are unprepared to cope with the growth. In situations like that you may have to invest more money than you expected to keep up with demand, hire more staff, and give over your daily life for a time to your burgeoning venture.

That's not to say that success isn't a great thing . . . or that failure is inevitable. All I am saying is that you need to look at every possible outcome before you jump into something. Either on paper (preferred) or just in your head, consider what would happen to your bank account if you a. failed, b. succeeded beyond your wildest dreams, or c. just plugged along. Then consider the impact on your life of those three outcomes. Your gut feeling will tell you when taking a risk is right. If the amount of money you are risking is low, trust your gut. Otherwise, be prudent and get an accountant or attorney to go over your numbers and projections with you. If you're investing with partners, be smart and check them out too. At least Google them and see what's on the Internet about them. You may want to have someone (your accountant or attorney probably) run a background check on them.

> *Look at every possible outcome before you jump into something.*

Do You Trust Them?

You'll also want to run a gut check on anyone you are considering taking a risk with. Use your intuition. A person who guarantees something that sounds too wonderful should not be trusted. The fact that someone is well-dressed or attractive doesn't say a thing about that person's trustworthiness. Neither does a beautiful office or a suave manner. Try to pick up on subtle clues that things may not be right. Are they trying to persuade you a little too hard? Do they play nervously with papers or their grooming? Most telling: Do you receive vague answers when you ask for specifics?

I was cheated out of $100,000 by some guys who were *mucho* slick and seemed to have all the answers when they asked me to invest in their business. I knew someone who worked there, and so I thought they could be trusted to use the money well. It turned out that they were on the brink of bankruptcy and used my money to keep the lights on for a few weeks. Then they went out of business, taking my investment with them. Now I trust my gut more when it tells me to look further into something. Unfortunately, at that time I was focused on the relationship these men had with my acquaintance and not on them or their proposition. My gut was giving me warnings that I failed to heed. Never again.

Does It Fit My Expertise?

I would never buy, say, a llama farm because I know nothing about those animals except that they spit. And I would never start a restaurant because I don't like to cook (although I love to eat). By sticking with opportunities in my field, I bring something to the table: a degree of understanding that actually *lowers the risk* I face. In my own fields, television and advertising, I know what a good operation looks like. Your own business ventures, investments, and career moves will be much more successful if you stick to what you know well, branching out only gradually, not taking huge leaps into the unknown. If you're a computer specialist, does that mean you shouldn't market your new idea for a revolutionary type of bra? Not at all. But if you want to lower the risk, you'll find a partner who knows a great deal about retail—or bras. Or at least join a support group where you can learn all you can, such as an industry trade group or a women's business development center.

Whether a big payout is likely depends heavily on how well your idea fits your customers' needs, whoever those customers may be. As an expert in the field, you can evaluate that fit precisely if you are honest with yourself. I recently used my expertise to become the majority owner of a BMW dealership. Do I know everything about cars? No. But I know a lot about selling to businesspeople, the kind of people who buy BMWs. Even in bad times successful people still buy luxury cars. *Por eso*, my investing in a BMW franchise is a lot less risky than it may look.

Is It Realistic?

Look for the "story" behind the idea you have or the proposal someone else is presenting. Does it seem likely that things will happen as predicted? In the case of Entravision, I had observed for myself that Spanish-language media (and the Spanish-speaking audience) was growing in California. Therefore, I believed my potential partners when they said that we would be well positioned to take advantage of that. But you must also look beyond the good story to the assumptions being made. Will your venture succeed only if the economy is expanding, for instance? Many venture capitalists who invested in dot-coms learned that what goes up does eventually come down. The business model that many of the dot-coms operated under just didn't make sense in bad economic times. In other words, look for the "backstory" to understand the level of risk you are being asked to take on.

Even when the risk is something as seemingly simple as changing jobs, make sure you evaluate the story you are being told carefully. A girlfriend of mine recently was offered a job at AOL/TimeWarner that would have required her to move across the country. It was a great offer and an exciting new job (high payoff), but my friend took the time to look into the offer and the division in detail before giving her answer. What she found scared her: massive layoffs and a company seemingly in financial disarray, although with vast financial resources. The job had a much higher level of risk, in other words, than she had anticipated.

Can You Negotiate Away Some Risk?

My friend could have run away screaming from the offer, but she didn't. Instead, she decided to reduce her risk before accepting the offer, the same thing I did with the Entravision deal. Before agreeing to take the job, she extracted an agreement from her prospective employers: They would guarantee that her job would not be cut for at least a year and that her moving expenses would be covered.

Why did they do that for her? That's easy. They already had told her they thought she was the best person for the job by making the offer. Therefore, she knew she had the *power position*, the most influence over the outcome of the negotiation.

Once you know that people need you more than you need them, you can negotiate away a lot of risk. Once people decide to buy your services, whether as an employee or as a business owner, you have more power than you realize. As soon as you know you are "it," you can start your campaign to receive the highest payoff for the least risk. How to do that? By negotiating *como un hombre*. Really. It works or the guys wouldn't do it.

The first step is to *know what you want*. Will more money induce you to take on more uncertainty? How much more money? Would other perks, such as a company car, make the risk more acceptable? Or would you rather negotiate about your job duties or working hours? Whatever you decide you need, ask for *every bit of it*—and a little more—up front and do it before your "opponent" makes an offer of his own. You can always negotiate down if you need to, but you'll never get more than what you ask for initially. When I moved to Providence to take the sales manager's job, I asked for a salary $10,000 more than I thought I was going to get, plus a car, a car phone, and moving expenses. And darned if I didn't get it all.

But what if you don't get everything you ask for? It's important to go into any negotiation armed with concessions, that is, *things you wouldn't mind giving up.* I wouldn't have minded, for instance, giving up the company car if I had been asked to. That was less important to me than the moving expenses and the salary. Prioritize your needs before you go into any situation where you are asking for something. Then you'll be sure to come out with the items that are most important to you.

Go into any negotiation armed with things you wouldn't mind giving up.

At this stage you also should make some guesses about *what the other party wants to end up with* as a result of the negotiation. If you think it through, you may be surprised to discover that what is important to you isn't at all important to the other side. An extra $10,000 either way may be just a drop in the bucket to a big corporation, for example. (So ask for $20,000!) Or you may be able to find out that your predecessor had a company car or free country club membership, perks that you can ask for too. (See why research ahead of time is so important?) You'll be ahead of the game if you try to figure out how to give the other party his or her top priorities while achieving what you want the most at the same time. By giving up something the other party wants, you show that you value an ongoing cordial relationship based on mutual respect. There is no reason you can't have a great relationship and a good deal, too.

It is also vital to have a *"walk-away."* Think about what you can live with and what you cannot. What is the absolute bottom line you'll accept? Be prepared to walk away if they can't meet at least those terms. Accepting less opens you up to anger, resentment, and a loss of self-esteem. The good news is that knowing your walk-away makes you a stronger negotiator. Any sign that you might break off talks often scares the bejesus out of the other side, who, remember, is already vitally interested in working with you. Concessions often come fast and furious once they know you would be perfectly happy *not* doing the deal. And yes, you should make sure they believe you will walk away even if you feel in your heart that this is the most important deal of your life. Acting—pretending to feel something you do not—sometimes gets you everywhere, darling.

Finally, you need to *get it in writing.* Whatever you agree to, send a detailed memo right away outlining your understanding of what you agreed to. If you can afford it and the amount of money involved is large, you may want to consult an attorney about the fine points. Get the other side to sign the agreement too. A verbal agreement will stand up in court, but a signed document is beyond argument. If anyone doesn't hold up her or his end, it is handy to be able to pull out a document and point to the relevant passage.

BEING UNAFRAID OF RISK

Minimizing risk as much as possible helps lower our fear of taking bold leaps, but it doesn't take it away completely. In our deepest *alma,* even when we look confident, we often are thinking "*¡Aye, Dios mío!* What am I doing?" We are naturally afraid of the unknown, of failing, of looking foolish. Everyone feels that way in moving beyond her comfort zone. But if you don't move into the unknown, you'll be stuck where you are and may be miserable. Still, fear of taking risks can be very difficult to overcome. That's why you need to train your inner *leona* to come roaring forward when you need her.

> *If you don't move into the unknown, you'll be stuck where you are and may be miserable.*

First, you must realize that it's very human to feel nervous or even fearful when you are trying new things. Successful women *accept that fear and move on.* Even better, they've learned how to use the rush of emotion they feel to energize their dealings with the world. I used to be terrified of public speaking until I realized that the audience was there because those people were *interested* in what I had to say. And who was I to let my fear stand in the way of letting my listeners profit from my experiences? After that I just got up and spoke from the heart, letting any lingering nervousness turn up the cha-cha of my presentation. In the process I learned that once you perceive your fear as something you can control (or ignore), it loses its power to defeat you.

> *Tune out advice that says why you can't do something.*
> Raydean Avecedo, *president and CEO, RCMI*

You also can minimize fear by having *a fallback plan.* I am always prepared to "exit stage left," as the cartoon character Snagglepuss used to say. That doesn't mean you shouldn't be fully committed to any plan of action. It simply means that in the back of your mind you have an idea of what you'll do if things don't work out. You don't need to be afraid of the worst-case scenario when you have a fallback. It becomes your *choice* to ride out any hard times that may come along—or to implement your fallback plan. Your plan doesn't have to be complex or completely developed, either. A friend of mine who has her own business always told herself that if the business didn't fly, she could always go back to work for someone else. That has been enough to reduce her fear and keep her in business for almost two decades.

> *You don't need to be afraid of the worst-case scenario when you have a fallback plan.*

Another way to get your *leona* to leap into action is by *taking baby steps*. Raydean Acevedo, the president of a Denver environmental consulting firm, told me once about her belief that fear can be a woman's greatest enemy. Her company has been involved in some huge environmental cleanups whose complexity could daunt anyone. Unknown wastes may have been dumped years ago by companies that have been taken over by others, but it was her company's job to get to the bottom of the problem and figure out who was responsible. Along the way she learned how important it was not to become so overwhelmed that she might be afraid to take on those well-paying jobs: "I try to take all the problems apart and deal with them piece by piece. A little piece of a problem is not scary at all."

Finally, the support of friends and family is extremely helpful in lowering your fear level even if they are not in favor of what you plan to do. Some of them will be afraid for you and warn you not to take on the risk. The best way to get them off your back? Show them why it's a good idea! Laying out your case repeatedly for different family members and friends will increase your confidence level. Pay careful attention, though, to anyone who criticizes specific parts of your plan, especially if that person has experience in your field. She or he may have good suggestions that will lower your risk even further.

> *Laying out your case repeatedly for different family members and friends will increase your confidence level.*

RISK IT ALL? THE REWARDS OF STARTING YOUR OWN BUSINESS

I have never actually started my own business. However, I know from the experience of friends and clients that it's one of the best ways to build wealth that was ever invented. It's also one of the easiest ways to lose your *camisa*.

Starting your own business may be your only option, however, if you've discovered that your *pasión* can't be fulfilled any other way. Mary Ann Padilla, president of Sunnyside Inc., a staffing firm in Denver, discovered early on that she didn't like working for a boss. She wanted to be in control of all the important decisions. But she started small, talking herself into a job at a placement agency. She worked her way up in that firm, learning all she needed to know, and then decided to open her own firm. Then she was stopped dead because she couldn't get a bank loan without a cosigner. Mary Ann, however, wanted to go it alone, to be in control.

She asked her brother for a loan to pay a couple months' rent and telephone bills in a small, inexpensive office. Her father made the office furniture and drapes. No fancy conference room and receptionist for her. Instead, she worked the phone hard, drumming up business and impressing potential clients with her nearly 24/7 commitment to solving their [the clients'] staffing problems. "I paid off my brother six months later," she exults. "By doing what I had to do—working long hours, joining organizations to network, speaking everywhere I could, meeting everyone—I made my business a success." She draws deep satisfaction now from sitting on the board of one of the banks that turned her down for a loan!

Maria Rodriquez, *una española* now living in Washington, D.C., says her success as a business owner comes from taking calculated risks and doing what she believes in. She started her company, Vanguard Communications, as a public relations advocacy firm for social causes including mental health, the environment, civil rights, and health issues. "Most of my employers since college have been driven by corporate goals," she says. "You might be promoting toothpaste or cigarettes whether you believed they were good products or not. It didn't take me long to realize how powerful this work is . . . unlike advertising, something that's seen in newspapers or on broadcast media is believed to be objective—even if someone's paying to be sure it gets in there. So if I'm going to do that, I'm going to do it for things I believe in."

Just 27 when she started Vanguard, Maria minimized her risk as much as she could by living with her parents. "At least I knew that if I failed, I would still have a roof over my head."

She also avoided risking everything she owned as her business grew. She refused, for instance, to mortgage the home she eventually purchased to buy out a partner. "Don't pledge anything unless you are willing to give it up," she wisely advises. She also advises taking out only short-term loans, with a payback period only long enough to keep your motivation high when you think about having to pay the loan back. Her approach seems to be working quite well. Fifteen years later her company has high-profile clients including the American Civil Liberties Union, Farm Aid, and the National Wildlife Federation. And Vanguard was nominated for public relations agency of the year by *PR Week* magazine in 2003.

If you feel business ownership is right for you, go for it. Many cities have Women's Business Development Centers that can give you advice on what you need to do to get business loans, grants, and special government contracts (called set-asides) for minority-owned businesses. Do your homework intensely before you consider quitting your job to go out on your own. There's nothing wrong with continuing to collect a paycheck while you plan for business-ownership success in your off hours.

A NEW KIND OF JOB SECURITY

Even if you are not interested in owning your own business, you can take an ownership interest in your career and become the CEO of your destiny. You just need the courage to give in to your entrepreneurial instincts, to listen to that little voice that says, "I know a better way." Ignore the pigeonhole your company tries to put you into. Dive feet-first into the opportunities that present themselves. Don't be afraid to ask "dumb" questions, especially if you are new. An outsider's perspective sometimes leads to brilliant new ways to get things done.

But why bother? Isn't it enough to do your job to the best of your ability? Well, look at it this way: If your boss needs to lay someone off, will it be the person who has demonstrated consistently that the company's success is important to her or the *chica* who just shows up in the morning and does her job? Taking ownership of your job has benefits far beyond simply holding on to it too. In terms of your own marketability, it makes a real difference to be able to say, "Here are some of the ideas I've come up with, and here's how my company profited from them." Having demonstrable results has allowed me to pick and choose jobs. And to be able to do that in this economy is a real luxury.

Still, who has time for all that? You do. A Chinese philosopher named Lao-Tzu once said, "Time is a created thing. To say 'I don't have time' is like saying 'I don't want to.'" Think hard about that the next time you feel you don't have time for something.

As I've said all along, everything falls into place when you concentrate, really concentrate, on what's important to your happiness and success. And because you are the "CEO of you," your most important task is to decide what your priorities are. Don't get caught up in easy but unimportant tasks. And *don't* obsess over perfection. *Perfección* never happens. It just makes women, especially Latinas, miserable. We try to do our best at everything and end up boiling with resentment because we have too much to do. I know. I tried to be perfect too.

Don't *obsess over perfection.*

We try to be supermoms too. Most of our husbands learned from their *mamís* that a woman who loves them will cater to them. Even if they've told you that they really want a marriage of equals, something inside of them expects to come home from work to a hot dinner on the table and a sparkling house. When it doesn't happen, they are puzzled and hurt, even if they don't quite know why. Others want no truck with this equality stuff and simply expect their wives to work a second shift at home.

What can you do about it? I've seen many successful businesswomen manage marriage and work quite well. They did that, it seems to me, by taking control of the situation, just as they would as CEOs of their own companies. First, they understood that their families were not mind readers. To get the help they needed, these women asked for specific behavior changes. In addition, they were prepared with reasons why that change in outcomes was necessary for smooth operations. They made certain to hold those discussions when everyone was calm, not pissed over some breakdown. And they decided what *they* could give up in return for more considerate treatment from other members of the "team." What does that sound like? Right, a negotiation. Why shouldn't your family benefit from the skills that could make you an excellent risk taker and bargainer at work? Among family is a good place to practice those skills. If you can negotiate your *novio* into picking up his socks himself, watch out, world!

4
Palabras Que Seguir: Words to Lead By

*S*ome women are born leaders of others; almost everyone else can learn to lead. You would not be reading this book if you did not at least have the potential to be a great leader. The best leaders can inspire others to perform at the highest level and work together to accomplish astonishing things. We Latinas tend to make the most effective leaders because we want everyone around us to be comfortable and content. We do not try to lead by intimidation or by using power plays. We want to create teams that work together to meet agreed-on goals. We do not care much for titles, only for what we can do with them. We want to give guidance, not orders.

> *Latinas are effective leaders because we want everyone around us to be comfortable and content.*

In essence, we want to re-create *la familia* at its best in our workplaces and civic organizations, except with ourselves at the head of the table. And I am here to tell you that the Latina way works, and works much better than do traditional power-oriented leadership methods. *Por ejemplo,* in my 12 years as a Univision station manager in Denver, I had virtually no turnover in my staff. Almost the only people who left were those I had groomed for better things. That type of record is not common in television, where jealousy and competition can tear apart a station. But because these ideas worked in that hard-charging environment, I am convinced that my leadership ideas can work anywhere.

A GREAT LEADER OR JUST THE BOSS?

Why is being a great leader so important when you are in charge? One word: Inspiration. Everyone wants to believe that the time he or she spends outside the home—a major chunk of our lives today—makes a difference. Leaders who do their jobs well give their followers the *inspiración* to achieve great things, and people who are led this way often are spurred on to accomplishments that they didn't think were possible. What great leaders do is inspire their followers to buy into the idea that their contribution is vital to the success of any operation. Once they do that, the people they lead are fired up to overcome any obstacles that get in their way.

> *Leaders who do their jobs well give their followers the* inspiración *to achieve.*

Sure, individuals can inspire themselves to greatness, and I've already told you some ways to do that in your own life. But someone must take charge if a group of people is going to achieve great things as a team or a company. Just like toddlers taking their first steps, lower-level employees need to be able to depend on someone to protect them so that it will be safe to take risks. Even experienced people need the occasional wind beneath their wings—assurance from someone else that their efforts matter. People also want to know that they have someone they can trust to give them an unbiased opinion. Generous leaders never seek to pit people against each other, but instead give honest feedback at all times because they know this kind of leadership fosters a productive environment. It also makes for a trusting place to live and work.

Leaders need to be able to deflect the heat from everyone else too. Someone has to step up, make the hard decisions, and live with the consequences. But great leaders also let others make most decisions on their own—and then live with the consequences of those decisions. Great leaders never seek to blame anyone for mistakes made under their watch. Instead, they know that giving people opportunities creates more good leaders and makes their companies and organizations even stronger. And *no*, they are not afraid to groom leaders among their subordinates who may take their place someday. Great leaders always have their eye on the next rung up anyway.

The best news is that Latinas have never been in a better position to become great leaders. Many more of us are in the middle-management pipeline to the top, and there are now more educational programs designed to help us learn how to lead. One is the National Hispana Leadership Institute (www.nhli.org), a program worth investigating by any ambitious leader on her way up. Christina Torres went through the program in 1999 and is now an assistant dean at Arizona State University. "Young Latinas today are in the same place that young *Anglas* were twenty years ago," she said recently. "We are just starting to make real progress in corporations, the academy, and nonprofits. One of my students, for example, is now doing a fellowship at Harvard. I know from my experience in the Leadership Institute that the more Latinas see other Latinas in leadership positions, the faster we all will advance." How's that for a reason to aspire to be a great leader?

Por eso, everyone knows that most bosses are *not* great leaders. You, I, and everyone we know have served under at least one boss who seemed to go out of his or her way to make work more difficult. And one only has to look at the sorry tales of Enron, Global Crossing, and MCI to find examples of corporate leaders who couldn't care less about anything except what's lining their pockets. In 2003 it was shocking to see how many Fortune 500 "leaders" gave themselves big raises even when employees were being laid off or being given wage and benefit cuts. This is hardly the way to inspire greatness. We are certain to see more corporate implosions like that of Enron because this kind of behavior leads to hollow companies staffed by people with no loyalty to anyone but themselves.

> *Young Latinas today are in the same place that young Anglas were 20 years ago.*

We all know a bad boss when we see one. Those bosses have ways of spoiling everything around them, usually because they don't care about anyone but themselves. And yes, they are usually *hombres*, but only because men still outnumber women in positions of leadership. There are plenty of women who let even the faintest whiff of power go to their heads. It's useful to look at some of the specific actions that turn some bosses into jerks so that we can avoid acting like them when we get into positions of leadership. Is your boss *aquí*? Are you?

> *There are plenty of women who let even the faintest whiff of power go to their heads.*

The Shameless Self-Promoter

This type of boss takes credit for every project and makes sure the world hears about it. He or she may even praise you in private, but higher-ups will never find out about your good work. According to this boss, nothing could have been done without him.

The Know-Nothing

This authority figure may have been promoted too fast or too far. He knows nothing about the work being done in his area and doesn't want to learn. He finds it impossible to communicate the needs of his people in decision-making meetings, and so they always get the short end of the stick. And because he knows so little but won't admit it, he constantly changes his mind about what he wants, usually long after he's sent you off in the opposite direction.

The Blamer

She blames everyone but herself for the failures of her team, usually at the top of her voice. As a result, she never learns what she could have done better. For her, the future only holds more opportunities to lay blame.

The Disrespecter

From *el Irrespetuoso*, you can expect to be treated like a disposable item bought at the 99-cent store. She can replace you easily with the next *Juana* off the street, she thinks, so why consider your feelings or needs?

El Mentiroso

The liar wants to get ahead any way he can. This type is extremely dangerous because he often tries to blackmail his subordinates into signing on to his schemes. Don't do it. You could end up facing criminal prosecution like the people who shredded documents for Enron. Tell someone in authority about this one. Or run.

The Egomaniac

This guy is in love with the sound of his own voice and his own pretty (or not so pretty) face. He's a "legend in his own mind." I saw this a lot in my television work. Whenever there's a camera around these guys, they try to get into the picture. This boss is not so much a threat to your career as a threat to your sanity. Who wants to listen to someone talk all day—mostly about himself? There are more important things to do. Xeroxing, filing, looking out the window—believe me, whatever you do is more important than listening to these bosses. Don't be a polite Latina and put up with it. Let them find someone else to talk the ear off of. Trust me, this boss won't even notice you're gone.

If you have to work with one of these jerks, determine how much you can tolerate and why it's important to you to put up with it. On my way up I had my share of bad bosses. Usually I stuck it out because the job would advance my career. In one case I was hired to be the subordinate of a woman who, as I found out later, had been given no say in hiring me. *Ay*, did she resent my presence. From day one she tried to get me fired. I did my best to develop a relationship with her. I often asked her out for lunch or coffee, but she always refused. She turned down all my ideas with a simple "We don't do things that way." I wasn't even invited to staff office parties. I did my job and worked on relationships with everyone else at that television station. (I became the CEO of my own career, in other words!) Eventually everyone trusted me more than they did her—and she was the one who got fired.

Unless you treat people well when you are a leader, you can be sure that what goes around will come around and bite you in the butt. It doesn't matter whether you supervise one employee or thousands or whether you are leading a volunteer group; you will come out on top—and stay there—if you always try to be the greatest leader you can be.

ANY LATINA CAN BE A GREAT LEADER

Within every *mujer* are the personal qualities that make people *want* to do their best work. Some of you simply haven't let the world see those qualities yet. Our culture has taught us valuable lessons that make us excellent managers of people. *Primero*, Latinas rarely bark orders and expect unquestioning obedience. That is what makes us so effective as leaders: We realize that everyone who works for us has a brain and wants to use it.

In addition, there are other cultural values that make it easier for people to follow us as long as we use them in the right way. For instance, I tried very hard never to let my position go to my head. *Mamí* said that nobody ever liked a rude person, *una persona grocera*, and I never let a promotion get in the way of being nice. I had jobs where the boss constantly talked down to employees or embarrassed them in front of others. That's not necessary, ever. You can take people aside to give them advice that you hope will help them. Reprimanding them in front of others is just disrespectful.

> *Being bilingual and bicultural is an asset. It is having twice as much as most folks.*
>
> Bettina Flores,
> *author of* Chiquita's Cocoon

I also never expected that just because it said *"La Jefa"* on the door, people were automatically going to *respetarme*. The fact that you can fire or promote someone doesn't mean that that person is going to be motivated to do her or his best work for you. In fact, says the author of *1001 Ways to Reward Employees*, "When [employees] are satisfied with pay and benefits, those elements are like wallpaper." The author goes on to explain that "if they have a good boss, they feel they have a good job. They want trust; they want to be shown that their opinions are valued, to be kept in the loop and to be supported in taking initiative." I agree wholeheartedly. I feel I am qualified to be *la jefa* only as long as I am helping my employees do their jobs.

A great leader is also extremely honest, *honrado*. The root of that word in Spanish is *honra* (honor), and our honor is indeed on the line when we lead. If our word means nothing, no one can ever trust anything we say. Once someone catches us in a lie, that person will always suspect us of having a hidden agenda or trying to get more than we deserve. If we lie, we are asking to be lied to by others. *Sí*, dishonesty seems to be part of corporate culture these days, but don't be tempted to give up one of our strengths as a Latina just to fit in. When you get right down to it, we Latinas hate bullshitters. I've discovered over and over that employees (and most higher-ups) appreciate honesty more than anything else. Is it really a surprise that the people who blew the whistle on Enron and the FBI were women? Not to me. Only honesty inspires loyalty; dishonesty means every woman for herself.

A great leader does not take no for an answer either. She is driven to question authority and always challenges "final" decisions that seem misguided. (Read: They stink.) That is, a great leader is courageous, *valiente*. She is not a "yes woman" (*mujer de sí*). Of course, you'll be slapped down—many times—for standing up for what's right. But a leader who is *valiente* expects that; she knows that it's part of her real work, *su trabajo fundamental*. If she is fighting for something important, she will never give up. That goes *doble* when she's fighting for her employees. Great leaders are not afraid to speak up, although they learn to choose their words with care as they climb the corporate ladder. As Latinas, we learn early on about the importance of saying just the right thing. It's a skill that serves us *muy bien* in the business world, too.

Finally, as a great leader you realize that people want to learn from your example. You must always be a model of the behavior you want to see around you whether you feel like it that day or not. Sick today? Fought with your *novio* last night? Forget it! Put on your lipstick and liquid concealer and put it out of your mind at work. People won't respect you if you tell them your troubles, even if they nod and say, *"Dígame más."* But at the same time a great leader makes it clear that outside of personal issues, absolutely nothing is off limits. In other words, your employees should feel free to question anything, to say anything, just as you do. As Valentina Garcia, the assignment editor for *Noticias Univision Colorado* and one of my former employees, said recently, "Leaders should be approachable. After all, how can leaders share their gift if no one will talk to them?"

OCHO WAYS TO BE A GREAT LEADER

It's all well and good to talk about the qualities of a great leader, but to make yourself into one, you need to learn some practical strategies as well. Here are eight that have worked their magic *para mí*.

Numero Uno: *Surround Yourself with Good People*

The most valuable thing a great leader does is admit she that doesn't know it all. Be honest with yourself about where your skills lie. Then search for employees who excel in your areas of weakness. For instance, I've always made sure my budget manager understood my dislike of numbers and knew to take the time to explain them to me thoroughly. Thankfully, good people are attracted by your honesty when you admit you are hiring them to be smarter than you are in certain areas. The key to keeping them is to continue to admit your dependence on them and regularly give them credit—in the presence of others—for making your job easier. At the same time, you also want to show them the way to advance from their current jobs. If they succeed in the company away from your influence, it is an excellent reflection on you, *no es?*

Numero Dos: *Set Inspiring Goals*

Too many workplaces set only one goal: to make money. And although it is necessary to make money to keep the doors open, this is not a goal that turns employees on. After all, they see that in most cases the lion's share of the money goes to top executives and shareholders. People faced with inspiring goals, in contrast, find that their work is easier because the focus shifts away from petty bickering and power struggles. Instead, what is paramount in everyone's mind is meeting the goal. How do you go about setting these inspiring goals? You ask your people: What is important to them? What would make them feel they are really contributing? Ask your employees to dream—in meetings with you or on paper—about what the company could accomplish and how they could help. Deep down, what people really want is to make a difference with their lives. Ask them to tell you how your company can help them do that and how your corporate goals can be expressed in those terms as well. Once you inspire the people around you, you'll find that they approach their tasks with an astonishing level of commitment.

Numero Tres: *Be Human*

Well, sure. How can you not? Unfortunately, staying real is hard to do in the upper reaches of corporateland. There's something about corporate culture that can suck the humanity out of any leader. At the most basic level being human as a leader means letting people know that you understand that they have a life outside work. It takes just a few minutes a day to catch up on the doings of your coworkers' families and day-to-day lives. Ask how Serafina's kid did in the baseball game last night or how José's mother is doing this week. Latinas are great at this sort of thing, yet there's often a real struggle in our souls over how to be caring and professional at the same time. The key is to be truly engaged and interested in what your colleague has to say but to keep your catch-up sessions short. (Always be on the way somewhere when you stop to chat.) If you remember what's happening in their lives from one conversation to the next, people will feel listened to and appreciated. Remember the kid's name, the husband's name, the dog's name even if you have to write everything down in your Palm Pilot and memorize it.

Numero Cuatro: *Be a Cheerleader,* una Porrista

No, you don't have to bring your pom-poms to work. (Although I'll bet some of you still have them!) You don't even have to do the splits, *¡gracias a Dios!* Cheerleading on the job is a lot less taxing than that. All you have to do is catch your employees or coworkers doing something well and praise them generously. Then tell the world about it.

But you need to be careful not to overdo it. Over the last twenty years or so the "self-esteem" movement in American schools has given praise a bad name. If every kid who plays on a team gets a trophy, what does a trophy mean to the kids who do really well? Praising an employee for doing his or her job correctly will result in merely adequate performances from many people: "Gee, if she thinks that was good, she doesn't know anything about this job." Top performers will not see proportional rewards for their extraordinary efforts and may quit trying so hard. Upshot: Being a bit too stingy with praise is better than being too generous. Save it for beyond-the-call work. But then make sure everyone knows, from the top of the company on down, through e-mail distribution or other forms of public recognition. Shout it from the rooftops if you have to.

However, you need to cheerlead *every* employee who is *not* making the grade. I have never waited for a performance review to notify an employee about a performance problem. I want to give the highest marks possible to every employee at review time, and so I prefer to counsel them well in advance. When I see people struggling with any aspect of their work, I ask them to tell me "the story" of what they're doing in that situation. That gives me insights into what they could do differently, but I try to restrain myself from solving the problem for them. Often I'll ask them to role-play the tough calls or brainstorm new approaches, or I'll try to teach them what they need to know without imposing my solution on them. It's amazing how many poor performers end up with brilliant performance reviews as a result of this approach.

Numero Cinco: *Protect Your Employees*

A respected leader gives her employees a heads-up if she knows someone has an eye on them or if the company is facing serious problems. There is no reason to keep secrets like that in a company that wants its employees to do their best. You are not airing company laundry in public; you are informing those whose lives could be affected by the secret in question. It's your duty. Enough said. *¡Basta!*

Numero Seis: *Open Your Door—and the Books*

I'm a great believer in open management, the practice of telling employees everything that goes on in the company. As a station manager and now as an auto dealership owner, I always share budgets as well as corporate targets and goals, particularly with the top members of my team. The reason is simple: If your people don't understand the details, they can't do their best to make an appropriate contribution. Requests for raises or more funding for innovative programs would fall on deaf ears, I knew, if those requests weren't backed by realistic numbers. Thus, I'd give my employees the numbers they needed and even coach them: "Here's how to present this to make sure it's approved." (My door is always open for employees who want to discuss other problems as well. More about this later.)

If you are not allowed to share corporate financial numbers and results with subordinates—or if the numbers are not shared with you—I have to wonder if you should be working for a company like that. Be prepared to agitate if you must to get access to complete information about your company. Make a pest of yourself if you have to. You are making the very reasonable claim that you can't manage your responsibilities effectively without full disclosure of the company's bottom line and all the rest of its numbers.

What if you don't understand the numbers that are shared with you? As I mentioned before, this was a big problem for me early in my career because I was not a CPA. But I knew I'd be left behind if I was too proud to admit that I was sometimes lost around numbers. I got a colleague who was in love with numbers to explain to me what everything meant and how I fit in. Because of confidentiality, your helper is almost certainly going to have to be someone who works in your company, not an outsider. Make friends with someone who spends his (almost always it will be a man) lunch hour staring at spreadsheets or talks about "running the numbers." And don't be afraid to ask "stupid questions" of that person. How else are you going to learn?

Numero Siete: *Fire People Well*

Of course, great leaders have to *hire* the right people. That's a given; that's basic. Just as a marriage matchmaker would, we find just the right person to match the job, one whose skills and personality will inspire the rest of the staff to "fall in love" and embrace the new person as part of the team. But even more important than making excellent hiring decisions is knowing how to *fire* people well. Too many people who want to be leaders are scared spitless of having to fire anyone. When they eventually get around to doing the dirty deed, the fallout messes up not only the person fired but the people left behind—and themselves as leaders. You have to be able to fire people without destroying them in the process.

One of the hardest things I ever did was the first time I fired someone. As a Latina, I'm *muchísma* aware that the person I'm going to fire has a family and bills and responsibilities. As a result, the first time I needed to do it, I agonized so long over a salesman's poor performance that the poor guy knew what was coming weeks before I did. In fact, he knew he was a poor fit in the job and was ready to go. The day I fired him, though, he was generous enough to give me the gift of a new attitude toward firing. He said: "It's not the people you fire that hurt you; it's the people you don't fire."

That is so true. You'll never build a strong team when your dedicated employees have to cope with coworkers who come to work only for a paycheck. That's why you need to be ruthless about weeding out poor employees, *ahora mismo*. Thankfully, poor employees have one thing in common and are easy to spot: They all give the impression of being the laziest people on earth. These employees just want to put in their time and go home. They are the ones who never volunteer an idea, constantly find fault, and never stay late unless they are forced to.

Unfortunately, two other groups share this set of bad behaviors: the demoralized and the confused. A demoralized employee is one who has seen a lot of layoffs or experiences constantly shifting corporate goals. He or she may just give up and start muttering, "No one cares what I do anyway, so how much can I get away with?" A confused one, in contrast, truly does not know what he or she is doing wrong. The good news is that both groups of apparently lazy employees will respond to intense, concerned counseling before you begin writing poor performance reviews to start the firing process. The demoralized will appreciate the fact that you care, and the confused will find the fog lifting. Both groups will respond to the attention with an improved performance. Anyone who doesn't respond is just bone lazy or in the wrong job and should be terminated as soon as humanly possible. The rest of your employees will thank you, *créemelo*.

Numero Ocho: *Communicate Like a Leader*

We Latinas are pros at communication. Unfortunately, when we start to climb the ladder, many of us don't know how to portray ourselves as *leaders*. We need to learn—or at least I did—how to seem powerful enough to get the job done without becoming known as a you-know-what. (*Sí*, a bitch.) When I first got myself out of the farm fields, though, seeming like a bitch was the least of my worries. I even had to learn how to ask for what I wanted in no uncertain terms. Many Latinas have this problem. Listen carefully to your *amigas y amigos* sometime. Latinas, even accomplished ones, tend to make requests rather than demands. They show, through their words, even if they are not conscious of it, that they care most about the feelings of others. Men, by contrast, tend to care most about getting the job done. They most often make statements that are direct and to the point. Typically, they are more focused on the task at hand than on the feelings of those doing the tasks.

Does that mean that Latinas will always be too concerned about the feelings of others to communicate effectively as leaders? Not at all. I believe that concern for others makes us better leaders than men are. Unfortunately, it is still men who make most of the promotion decisions. And we will always have male subordinates who expect us to earn their respect by demonstrating absolute authority over them and brilliance at our jobs before they will do their best work for us. Therefore, we must be strong and demanding in many situations if we want to be considered for leadership positions by the men in our organizations. But what do they say (or think) when we are assertive? That's right: the dreaded B word again. It's one of the games men play to call us bitches, *perras*, when we try to move ahead. To many men, and some women, being called a bitch isn't really an insult since business is a game of winners and losers. Such ruthlessness is only a tactic aimed at highlighting the weaknesses of an opponent. Since you're going to be considered a bitch anyway, should you just go ahead and be one when you lead? *No*. There is a better way.

"Honor Your Inner Bitch"
In other words, you can lead in a people-centered way without giving away a bit of power. You can be assertive without being aggressive. You can be kind without being a pushover. When you "honor your inner bitch," you realize that you can have an inner core of steel without being hard on the outside. In fact,

the most powerful women I know are also some of the nicest people I know, but no one can ever take advantage of them. They would never think of relying on fear to keep employees "in line." Instead, they aim to create an environment where people really are the top priority rather than just another management training slogan.

One of the founders of Yahoo! said it perfectly, I think. "The most powerful force in business isn't greed, fear or even the raw energy of unbridled competition. The most powerful force in business is love," writes cofounder Tim Sanders in his 2002 book *Love Is the Killer App*. The way you go about communicating that love will create a loyal, creative, and productive workforce around you. The way you communicate your inner core of steel—your absolute confidence in the rightness of your course of action—determines how far and fast you will rise in your career. And when love and confidence are combined, they produce the mother of all leaders: the strong, respected woman.

> *I feel that as a leader I must keep creating leaders. We must create spaces where leaders come up and give them space to develop.*
>
> Rocio Saenz, *president, Local 615, SEIU*

TALKING TO UNDERSTAND . . . LISTENING TO CONVINCE

So how do you communicate your strength, especially when you're not yet *la jefa*? It's relatively simple, *jefita*, once you've practiced it a bit. You just need to get in touch with your inner bitch while staying true to your heart. That way you'll communicate exactly what you need to succeed at the same time that you build mutually beneficial relationships with those who hear you.

Here's a quick *cha-cha* through the communication skills that have served me best in persuading people to respect me, starting from the days when I managed to sell TV time to business owners who called me a "dirty Mexican" the first time I visited their stores. Communicating with people like that convinced me that I could always use my mouth and my ears to win. Everything after that was easy. Let's call them talking points, or *puntos de plática*.

Punto de Plática 1: *Take Up Space*

When you enter any room, you must learn how to attract positive attention to yourself. Don't do it with flashy or low-cut clothes but with an attitude that says "I've arrived." Introduce yourself to the first person you see in a room and everyone you don't know after that. Jump into conversations at the slightest opening with a humorous comment that relates to your business connection to the event. Stand up straight, letting your arms be loose and your shoulders relaxed. Lean in, smile, and touch. Soon people will be introducing you to others or coming over to find out what all the *risas* are about.

Punto de Plática 2: *Talk the Talk*

Like the ad says, "People judge you by the words you use." Fair or not, you need to clean up your speech in order to be respected as a leader. Many ambitious women (and men) hire voice coaches to lose their accents. As manager of the U.S. Hispanic Practice at the ad agency Burston-Marsteller in Dallas, Sara Lora has coached many business leaders to speak on camera: "I tell them that people don't notice your words but how you say things. Your pronunciation must be impeccable—whether in

English or Spanish—in order to inspire confidence." Sara should know: She talked her way into a radio news gig at age 12 in her native Puerto Rico. For that she credits her grandfather, who made her read the newspaper aloud every day to the tune of his precise corrections. You can do the same thing with a cheap handheld tape recorder and a critical ear of your own if you don't want to go to the expense of hiring a voice coach. In my opinion, though, it's well worth the money. I know how hard it was to stop saying "member" when I meant "remember." And I was born in the United States.

Punto de Plática 3: *Admit Your Mistakes Even If They're Not Yours*

The hardest thing in the world to say is "I was wrong." It's also one of the most useful phrases in business. Admitting a mistake immediately allows you to get past blame and start working on solutions. Allowing a mistake to fester only distracts your team from learning to do things better in the future. In fact, you should always take the blame for errors made by your subordinates. Doing that demonstrates by example that you are more interested in improvement than in finding scapegoats. Of course, if you know who screwed up, you'll want to counsel that person in private to prevent repeat performances. Once you've done that, though, just move on. Dwelling on mistakes only makes negativity the attitude people associate with you.

Punto de Plática 4: *Set the Stage for Victory*

If you go into any business situation unprepared, you'll get pushed around no matter how well you communicate verbally. But you can do a lot with symbols if you remember how powerful they are. I remember an occasion when I was trying to sell airtime to a Burger King franchise. I spent days preparing a presentation to impress the prospective client with our station's ability to reach his customers. I could have bustled into the conference room with my visuals and just presented them, but I chose to impress him in another way first: I got there way early and was calmly reading the business section of the newspaper in the conference room when he arrived. He told me later that my aura of calm and dedication to business raised me to another level in his eyes. And yes, he bought airtime. Never underestimate the power of a symbolic gesture.

Punto de Plática 5: *Speak Body Language*

Our bodies speak volumes for us whether we are aware of it or not. As author Lilian Glass, Ph.D., observes in *I Know What You're Thinking: Using the Four Codes of Reading People to Improve Your Life*, "The body tells you a great deal about yourself and others. Gestures, posture, and body position mean something because these signals are the body's attempt to bring suppressed feelings to the surface." In other words, you can enhance your ability to communicate simply by being aware of the body signals of others—and by being conscious that the signals you're sending may be at odds with your intentions. We Latinas, for instance, learn early on that looking down is a sign of respect or modesty. It took me a while to realize that I was sabotaging my authority by looking at the floor in stressful situations. I had to make a conscious effort to look each person in the eye when I spoke in order to convey respect for and interest in that person.

You body may be sabotaging you too. Spend a few minutes every day observing yourself and others to figure out what's being said subconsciously. Are arms or legs crossed, bodies angled toward doors, feet tapping, eyes darting around the room? This is a person who's shouting (silently), *¡Aye!* Get me out of here! Case in point: During the Iraq War I saw a televised meeting between President Bush and Russian Prime Minister Putin in which Putin was leaning so far away from Bush that I thought he'd fall off his chair. It was not very likely that Putin believed what he was hearing from Bush about those elusive weapons of mass destruction. You need to observe the signs of negative reactions in yourself and others carefully and react accordingly. In these situations you can relieve negative feelings with positive body language: Face the person straight on, lean forward, tilt your head or nod, and uncross your arms. Sometimes you can see people relaxing when you make these moves.

Punto de Plática 6: *Know Who Is Listening*

Whenever you speak, with one person or thousands, know something about your audience. If your group is small enough, ask a question that will give you insight into their needs. "What brings you here today?" is a simple and direct question that often gives you a lot of information. Why is this step necessary? To communicate well, you have to go where your listeners are and bring them along with you to your point of view. You must start from their experience and attitudes in order to persuade them to see things your way. They won't care about your message unless you do that. Understanding exactly who they are allows you to tweak your message to fit both the experience and the attitudes of your listeners. Focusing your message in this way conveys that you are interested in relating to your listeners as people, which is an essential trait for a good leader.

Punto de Plática 7: *Listen with Your Heart*

Latinas tend to be good listeners, but leaders develop those skills to the highest degree. Listening is vital to success, in fact, because it allows you to figure out exactly what people want.

Once you understand that, you can help them give you what *you* want in exchange. An understanding gained through listening also allows you to speak with a great deal more authority, knowing you are unlikely to be tripped up by details you assumed you understood. Unfortunately, even we Latinas are often too busy trying to talk about our own concerns or think about what we will say next to really listen.

Active listening, really hearing what others are saying, is an essential skill for great leaders. But it is *muy difícil*, at least at first, because it requires an intense focus on another person when our natural tendency is to focus on ourselves. It requires practice. I recommend that for the next week or two you try to have at least one active listening session a day for ten minutes—longer if you can stand it—until you get the hang of it. Don't tell the person you're practicing with until it's over. I'll bet she'll tell you what an exhilarating experience it was to be really heard for a change. Here's all you need to do.

- Don't interrupt. At all. No matter how important your thought is. Write it down if you have to and share it later. Apologize if you do jump in.

- Comment on the speaker's thoughts rather than giving an example featuring yourself. Personal examples are (perhaps unconsciously) intended to shift the conversation away from the person you are listening to and onto yourself.

- Indicate that you are listening by nodding or interjecting soothing seminonsense sounds (uh huh, tell me more).

- Don't change the subject.

- Don't give advice.

- Sit back and be comfortable and just listen.

When do you get to talk? Well, in these practice sessions, not a lot. Your only contribution should be to comment on the other person's thoughts without giving advice. Once you've mastered the fine art of listening, you'll be able to wait quite a while to talk because you've seen how effective active listening is for gathering the information you need to be a better leader. Also, you'll be able to interrupt more effectively if you happen to get cornered by a windy talker because you do it so rarely now. Even the long-winded may be surprised into shutting up when a noninterrupter interrupts.

Punto de Plática 8: *Be a Flirt*

People are charmed by people who listen to them. They are even more positive about people who flirt with them. I'm an equal opportunity flirter, in fact. I'll tell an 80-year-old woman that she looks *muy linda* or has great hair. I'll tell a guy how his tie reflects his eyes. And I'm a hugger too. When people put their hands out to shake, even at a business meeting, I'll often say, *"¡Por favor!"* and give them a big hug instead. (Sometimes, of course, even *I* have to tone it down. In a really serious business meeting I may only squeeze your arm while I shake hands rather than giving you a full-out hug. But that's what I prefer to do.) I want people to perceive me as warm, caring, and *interested* in them. There is no better way to do that than to flirt—in other words, to give people the gift of your full and undivided attention.

Punto de Plática 9: *Be Yourself*

Sounds obvious, I know, but stick with me here. Many *mujeres* believe that to rise in their companies they need to put on an act, to become just like the men. In my opinion, these *mujeres* are doomed to fail as leaders because people don't like fakers. That is an opinion shared by Candy Deemer and Nancy

> *Always excel, be humble, and carry your own tune.*
>
> Regla Perez Pino,
> Latin American specialist

Fredericks, high-ranking executives and authors of the wonderful *Dancing on the Glass Ceiling*. "No wonder so few of us have risen from middle management, where we are ever more populous, to the top executive ranks. We have forced ourselves to undergo a sort of psychic sex change—to become rough, analytical, rational, and unemotional—thinking that these male traits of leadership would be the key to the top-executive ranks. We believed that if we could just *fit in*, we could succeed. Well, we were wrong. Because true leaders do not worry about fitting in. They stand out and lead!" So stand out. Use your femininity and charm. Or kick ass and take names. Whatever your style is, go for it. Trust your instincts, call on your inner bitch (or goddess), and never fake it.

Punto de Plática 10: *Lead, Just Lead*

All the techniques in this chapter will make you a much more assertive communicator and possibly an astonishingly effective leader. But when you honor your inner bitch in this way, you soon realize that some people will always interpret assertiveness the wrong way. In their minds you are a controller, a manipulator—dare I say it, a ballbuster. You cannot change those attitudes. You can only let them roll off you like water off a duck's back. Or you can change minds. Day after day, from now on, show everyone around you what a great Latina leader looks like.

5
Pathways to Power: Finding Help on Your *Viaje*

*H*ere's the dirty little secret of success: Nobody cares whether you do your job perfectly every day. It's all about who you know—and whether those people like you. Your connections with the movers and shakers in your field will determine how far you go and how much money you will make, *absolutamente*. What is not so well understood by many Latinas is just how *fácil* it is to meet powerful people. Even if you are just starting out, you can begin plotting right now how you will meet people at the highest levels of your profession. No matter how long you've been in business, you can get farther by going out of your way to meet important people. When you make an effort to become known, it's almost unbelievable how quickly everyone learns your name and how far that name recognition can carry you. Who would have thought that a poor migrant worker like me would meet *el presidente* of Mexico? Not me, that's for sure.

> It's all about whom you know—and whether those people like you.

That brings me to the second dirty secret: Old-fashioned networking doesn't work very well if you want to get close to powerful people. Even if you introduce yourself to 10,000 people this year, you may not be any closer at year's end to the special people you need to meet. You will, of course, have met some very fine people, but if a majority of them won't remember you five minutes from now, what have you accomplished with all the time you spent meeting them? Not much. To make an impression on anyone, you need to find ways to stand out and be memorable. To gain entrance to the very highest circles, you need to be very clear about what will make you *una estrella* (a star) in the eyes of the people you want to meet.

What will make you a star? One thing and one thing only: *You must do everything you can to help other people.* It's as simple as that. It bears repeating: You become a star by forgetting about your own needs and concentrating on helping the people around you get what they want. This is networking with a twenty-first-century twist, so far beyond forcing your business card on someone that it isn't funny. Let's call it deep connecting, or *conexión profunda*. The basis of deep connecting, and the reason why it will be so good for your career, is that if you send your heart out into the world, it will come back to you multiplied many times over. People, especially powerful ones, love to help people they see helping others.

You must do everything you can to help other people.

And that's the key to successful deep connecting: It's networking without the element of greed and neediness. Old-fashioned networking asks, "What can you do *para mí?*" Deep connecting networking wonders always, "What can I do *para los otros?*" Focusing on others makes networking a lot easier for most women. They don't have to concentrate on pushing themselves forward but instead can concentrate on building webs of, well, deep connection. And that's a more comfortable place to be. By focusing outward unselfishly, you become known as a person who makes things happen. You become the center of a wheel of deep connections where everyone is grateful to you for making something happen in his or her life. And grateful people tend to have the objects of their gratitude foremost in their minds when new opportunities come along, especially if you are conscientious about keeping in touch. What could be more enhancing to a career than having other people constantly on the watch for opportunities to help *you*?

Old-fashioned networking, in contrast, often has more in common with telemarketing than with building relationships with people. Telemarketers call as many people as they can, as fast as they can, to tell them about the great product they have to offer. We hate the fact that they can't pronounce our names and don't care whether we need their product. Old-fashioned networkers elicit the same response. Business leaders have, in fact, learned to be extremely wary when they encounter networkers whose sole aim is to advance themselves. That's why the concept has such a "last century" feel to it. But we, as Latinas, have seen the deep connecting type of networking going on our whole lives. Our parents had a web of relatives and friends who felt at ease asking each other for help, and *los papás* always went out of their way to help certain individuals. To become stars in business (or academia or politics, etc.), we need to re-create those warm, loving networks of individuals who want the best for us and then make sure those deep connections attract the big fish swimming in the ponds where we aspire to swim.

> *We Latinas have seen the deep connecting type of networking going on our whole lives.*

In other words, the idea is to encourage the movers and shakers to come to us. As I mentioned earlier, I got the chance to invest in Entravision because I knew someone, who knew someone, who knew my partners-to-be. But if I hadn't impressed my first contact with my helpfulness and resourcefulness, I never would have been told about the deal that later made me rich. My eventual partners came to me because I "knew everyone" in Spanish-language television, even though, practically speaking, I didn't. But I made it my business to know people who knew people at the upper reaches of my profession, and eventually my reputation became known to them too. Deep connecting has a lot in common with a term that's come out of e-commerce in the last few years: *viral marketing*. Companies that engage in viral marketing try to create a buzz about their products by making them interesting to talk about. Similarly, with deep connecting you are aiming to create a buzz about how useful you are to have as a contact. Once you are able to plant *that* notion in the brains of several influential people, you will be able to inspire those people to help *you* and will have recruited the "tour guides" you need on your *viaje* to success. And what do tour guides do? The best ones introduce you to "the natives," the powerful people you need to meet and impress to get ahead.

> *No one can do it alone. Somewhere along the way is the person who gives you that job, who has faith that you can make it. And everyone has something to work with, if only she will look for it.*
>
> Grace Gil Olivares,
> *Latina activist*

MAKING DEEP CONNECTIONS: HOW TO GET LUCKY

I know that people wonder how I could have been so "lucky" to advance so far from my poor background. Some people even say it to my face. After all, not too many *muchachas* who start out sweating in the fields end up with fifteen-carat diamonds and 300 pairs of shoes. But *mujeres* who started out with a lot more advantages than I did can end up trapped in boring, repetitive jobs that do not stretch their minds—or their bank accounts—if they do not actively take advantage of everything life offers. I am convinced that I made my own luck through my belief in the power of deep connections. I also believe that any woman can do the same thing. All it takes is a commitment to being of service to others.

Yes, it takes time to be useful to others, but your time will be rewarded many times over. Will you see positive results right away? Maybe not overnight, but almost certainly, sooner rather than later, you'll start seeing positive changes if you work hard enough. But how do you find influential people and connect with them, especially if you are one of those—half the population—who are shy about meeting people? I want to share with you some of the tricks I learned along the way for setting off a spark in people and making a deep connection.

Be a Friend

It may surprise you to learn that I used to be one of the shy ones. To get over it, I decided to view everyone in sight as if he or she already were my friend. As with my friends, I would always greet everyone with enthusiasm. I would smile and say *hola* to everyone I met, from the janitor on up. I wanted then—and still want now—for everyone to go away smiling after they meet me. I want everyone to know me as Rico or at least *la mujer con la sonrisa linda* (the lady with the pretty smile). When you are friendly to everyone, the worst you'll get is the cold shoulder, and really, do you want to know that kind of person anyway? Most people will be supremely grateful (there's that word again) that you noticed them because everyone wants to be acknowledged. At big events, half the people who attend are afraid no one will talk to them and the other half are trapped by a bore they'd give anything to get away from!

Even if you are not at an event, talk to everyone everywhere. You never know where an important contact is going to come from. Take the time to talk to everyone you meet in line or in church. Look for opportunities to be where people gather. I've taken sailing lessons, volunteered to work with abandoned pets, gotten involved in the PTA. Heck, I've even been known to "work my dog." My little Yorkie, Inre, is so cute that people will strike up a conversation with me just to get a chance to cuddle him. I'm also one of those people who talk to everyone they sit next to on an airplane. Hey, it works! I've met two VIBs that way (VIB = very important boyfriend). And I've made hundreds of business and personal contacts, while having a blast along the way.

I also use deep connecting to gather information I can use later. *Por ejemplo*, to gain the attention of *los dueños* (company owners) or upper management, you need to find out what their interests are, especially outside of work. Most will be glad to have an opportunity to talk about something other than day-to-day business concerns, particularly if you can find common interests. Forget about impressing the bigwigs when you get a chance to meet them. Just chat.

Be "Charming"

Want to forget about your nervousness? Concentrate on making other people feel welcome. Be someone people want to be around. Susan RoAne, networker extraordinaire and author of *How to Work a Room*, counsels that the best approach is to try to be the nicest person in any room: "People remember the people who make them feel special, comfortable and conversant, and whose demeanors make them smile." You'll never have to bring, do or wear attention-getting gimmicks again! Nice is good . . . and memorable. Nice means asking questions of everyone you meet and really listening to the answers without being hurt if people don't return the favor and ask about you. Many people these days can't see beyond their own noses, but they'll think you are brilliant if you merely listen to them.

If you're shy, don't worry. People adore talking about themselves—and the people who give them the space to do so. Just ask a couple of questions about their work, and most people will be off and talking. You'll be learning a lot about the person who is spouting off—and evaluating whether he or she could be a valuable contact, worth spending more time getting to know. A friend of mine once sat next to the CEO of a small company on a flight from Chicago to Denver. By the time they landed, the man had offered my friend a job just because she listened to his business woes sympathetically.

Express Your Admiration with Chapter and Verse

This works particularly well with people you have known previously only by reputation. Well-known people are used to being fawned over but rarely get singled out for praise for specific triumphs. Supposedly, they are beyond needing such encouragement, especially from those lower on the totem pole. I know from experience that that is absolutely not true. We never grow out of our need for sincere praise for a job well done. Make sure your praise is sincere because phony praise can be smelled a mile off. Tell the people you admire precisely why you esteem them so highly and you'll make a deep connection. They'll be especially impressed when you don't ask for anything in return for your praise.

Have Conversations

One other advantage of deep connecting: You'll expose yourself to new ideas and perspectives. If you're not striving like heck to "network," you'll be able to have actual conversations with people. Ask provocative questions to get the ball rolling: What's the most exciting development in your field lately? What would you change about your work if you could? What's the most fascinating book or TV show you've seen lately? In my opinion, you can even talk about politics or religion even though our parents thought that was totally out of bounds for polite conversation. Talk radio and political television shows have given almost all people opinions they are aching to express. You may be surprised to find out who agrees with you and shocked at how much you come to enjoy introducing people with contrary opinions to each other.

Make Introductions

At meetings or charitable events, to avoid getting stuck for an extended time with an individual, introduce that person to someone else you know after no more than ten minutes. Do this even if it's someone you met fifteen minutes ago or someone you don't know at all who is just walking by if you're desperate to get away from a bore. But even if your conversation is fascinating, move on after ten minutes. You want to leave people wanting more—not less—of you. If possible, introduce your current companion to someone it will be useful for that person to know. If you've been proactive in your conversation, you should know enough about that person to do so.

You should also try to make as many useful introductions—otherwise known as referrals—as you can outside the context of business or social gatherings. Referrals are one of the best ways to make deep connections with people because the relationships you help establish can have a measurable effect on other people's lives and livelihoods. Unfortunately, too many people are reluctant to make referrals because they've been burned by them in the past. What excuse can you make when someone you've referred produces shoddy work, turns out to be a troublesome employee, or otherwise reflects badly on your judgment in making the introduction? I have been burned in that way, but I've tried not to let it make me shy about introducing people.

But it has forced me to make referrals "with a disclaimer." I call the person in my network who will be the recipient of the referral and say, "I'm going to refer someone to you because I think you can help each other a great deal, *but I'm not sure.* Just because the referral comes from me, don't feel obligated to do business with them or even spend too much time with them if the fit doesn't seem right." I then go on to tell them why my instinct tells me that they will be good for each other. I thus haven't guaranteed results, yet I've given them the reasons why I think this might turn into a good relationship. It's important to do both to ensure that your referrals don't crash and burn, which makes you look foolish. Don't let the fear of that outcome make you avoid the possibility that you could make two people exceptionally grateful to you, people who will be exceptionally alert for ways to help you in the future.

Gather Business Cards

I always have tried very hard *not* to give my business card to people unless they beg for it. Instead, I make it my business to get *their* cards, along with enough information about them so that I have the possibility of helping them in the future. As

I talk to people, I try to jot down information about them on the cards they give me so I that can remember it when an opportunity comes up. Then I enter it all in my contact management system as soon as I can after meeting people so that I don't lose it. (Thank heavens for modern technology. This is so much better than dealing with all those little pieces of paper—*Ay!*) Getting a business card also prevents me from forgetting names, something I'd do in an instant if I didn't collect those cards. Once you get a business card, try to use the name several times in your first conversation and then use it to follow up. Enough repetition usually seals a name even into my brain, but if I forget the next time we meet, I always admit it and plead (*con humor*) for forgiveness.

Follow Up Fast and Slow

When you meet someone *you want to stay in touch with*, it's important to contact that person again right after your first meeting. E-mail is ideal for this, and I wish it had been invented many years ago. No more than twenty-four hours after meeting someone, no matter how much other work you have to do or how tired you are, send a brief, friendly e-mail about the place where you met, the people you talked to together, something you witnessed at the event, or some business-related factoid or tip. If at all possible, pass on something relevant to your conversation with the person, but this may be impossible in a first e-mail. (*Por eso*, you may have nothing relevant handy.) At a minimum, though, you need to make the point that your meeting with your new contact was important to you and that

> *Don't take anyone for granted. Do things for people without thought of reward.*
>
> Juanita Chacon,
> *real estate broker, Denver*

you'll be trying to help that person whenever you can. That's all you need to do with most contacts.

For people you want to build a deep connecting relationship with, you also need to think about when your next contact should be. You need to stay in touch regularly, although you certainly don't have to establish a rigid schedule. I never could. I just contacted people when the spirit moved me. Still, you will get even better results than I did if you keep a list of your important contacts. Put them in a contact management program if you have one—and if you don't, why not?—and write down the week or day during which you want to make contact with each person again. You can follow up by sending an interesting article, calling with a referral, or sending a casually friendly e-mail, perhaps with a link to a terrific new Web site. But whatever you do, don't become an imitation spammer. Never put your important contacts on a mass mailing list and *never* forward jokes. You want your contacts to think of you as a thoughtful individual, not *una idiota* with too much time on her hands.

Keep in touch with important people and they'll begin to remember your name and then begin to help you make the connections you need to advance your career. I once heard about a woman who wanted to be published in *Cosmopolitan* magazine. She kept sending her ideas to an editor there and made sure to send out another idea as soon as she got a rejection letter for a previous one. She would even *thank* the editor for responding to her idea so quickly even though the editor's reply was always "no, thanks." The writer's goal was to have her name perpetually in front of the editor. Her name eventually became so familiar to the editor that the editor felt comfortable assigning her a story to write, which led to a column in the magazine, every writer's dream. All this happened because the writer kept in touch and kept it personal.

Show Some Appreciation Every Day

I send a token whenever I notice that someone has accomplished something. If I see your name in the paper and you are on my contact list, I will send you a bouquet or a handwritten personal note by mail (not e-mail). Even if you are a stranger but are a person I'd like to meet, I will acknowledge your achievement. Believe me, people remember your name when you've given them a pat on the back. So few people go even an extra inch to hand out recognition to others.

◆

CAREER RESOURCES

- **CareerWomen.com**

  A career advice and job bank site for women. Woman-owned.

- **Diversity, Inc.**

  www.HispaniCareers.com/JobSearch.html

  An executive search firm specializing in diversity recruitment. Accepts résumés from Hispanic candidates.

- **Empleo.com**

  Spanish-language job search and career advice site.

- **Coach.com**

  www.findacoach.com. Find a career or personal coach or become one.

- **iHispano.com**

  Search professional jobs by keyword, company, or state.

- **iMdiversity.com**

Site promises to match you with a "diversity-sensitive employer." Also sponsors a "Hispanic-American Village" with forums and links to inspirational articles.

- **LatPro.com**

Calls itself the largest job board for Hispanics. Can search by specialty, language proficiency, and a number of other qualifications.

- **Saludos.com**

Job search engine for bilingual (and other) jobs nationwide.

- **SpanUSA www.spanusa.net**

An executive search firm specializing in bilingual job placement.

Carolyn See, novelist and author of *Making a Literary Life*, recommends going a step further by sending one thank-you note a day to people who affect your life. She suggests that thank-you notes be sent to writers you admire, teachers who pushed you in the right direction, and people who touched your life in some way. For the purposes of creating deep connections with powerful people, though, I would take this wonderful suggestion in a different direction: Send thank-you notes to businesspeople whose ideas you admire, especially those who live in your city or town. Did you hear a speech that motivated you? Read an informative story about someone's company in the paper? Attend a meeting with an interesting lunch companion? Thank those people, one a day. If most of those thank-you notes are directed to people in your local area, your name will get around in a positive way, especially if you also offer to help those people with projects they mention in your presence. Make sure, though, that those offers of help are sincere and will fit into your life if they are accepted. Nothing reflects worse on you than having to say, "Oops, I don't have time for that after all!" after you've offered to help.

Send one thank-you note a day to people who affect your life.

Go Where Powerful People Are

Why is a *chica* like me schlepping around a golf course every chance I get? Well, by now I do it because I always hope I'm going to play a round one day the way Tiger Woods does. But back in the early days of my career I would have told you that a wood was what my dining table was made of and a dogleg was attached to a hound. It took one of my managers to convince me that only on the golf course could I level the playing field between myself and the guys with whom I was trying to do business. He must have been persuasive because I didn't even go home after work that day but went to Nevada Bob's to sign up for lessons.

And wouldn't you know it, that man was also right about how much golf can help a *mujer* meet top people, both men and women, these days. All you need to do is offer most people a game and they're ready to play. On the course you get their undivided attention—a ringing cell phone is considered the height of rudeness. And you learn a lot of snippets about their personalities, businesses, and tastes, knowledge you can put to work later on. Best of all, you develop a comfortable level of interaction, especially if you let them know you are out to *kick their butts*. Golfers appreciate the honesty and the challenge. You don't have to be physically fit or even very good at the game. Most people who play aren't. "Play lots a' golf" would be my foremost advice if you want to get to know the power brokers in your town.

In addition to golf (or instead of it, but don't be such a scaredy-cat, *miedosa*), join groups in which you are likely to meet the influential people in your town. Look in the newspaper for photo spreads of charity events that raise money for causes in which you are interested. Or look for announcements of community meetings. Try anything that interests you but stay on the lookout for people who seem to have a lot of power to get things done. You don't have to be wealthy to join most of these groups, merely willing to work hard for the cause. Make-a-Wish Foundation, for example, advertises on its Web site for volunteers to help grant wishes to kids with serious illnesses, but its membership is filled with people who donate hefty sums each year and are some of the best-connected people in every city in which the group operates. There is no better way to get to know the fat cats than to offer to help them make good use of some of that money. Once you have proved your worth at the service-delivery level, find out how you can get involved in the administration of the group; that often will lead to an offer of a seat on the volunteer board.

Try anything that interests you but stay on the lookout for people who seem to have a lot of power to get things done.

You can quickly become known in your profession, too, by volunteering for work that your association needs. Can you set up a conference? Recruit members? Raise funds? Whatever you can do, your professional association will welcome your help. Too few members always do the *leona's* share of the work and will be thrilled if you offer to help. Again, if you perform your assigned tasks in an outstanding way, you probably will be invited to join the leadership group. Do it. If you are on the board of your association, that is the absolute best way for a large number of people in your industry to get to know you and your abilities.

You may be thinking: "Surely it's more *difícil* than that to get into the inner circle." For the most part I have found that it is not difficult at all even *before* you become wealthy. Board members recognize the value of people who keep their promises, do the work they said they would do, and don't look at any task as being "beneath them." You need to be sure you never take on any task that you can't complete by the deadline because that will kill your leadership chances in a heartbeat. After you've completed a few tasks (or before), ask to join a board subcommittee and attend a few meetings. (Nonprofit board meetings must be open to the public except when sensitive issues are discussed.) You'll soon find your interest rewarded with greater responsibility. And if it isn't, you'll know it's time to find a more promising group.

How will you know if a group is worthy of your efforts?

1. The group supports a cause or goal that inspires you. You must be passionate about what the group does or you will not be willing to give the extra effort that committed volunteering requires. Realize that you are offering to give up part of your precious weekend or evening downtime to get involved. The mere desire to meet influential people will not be enough to sustain your commitment.

2. You enjoy the people you meet at the group's functions. Snobby people aren't going to become easier to

deal with once you get to know them. In fact, it's just the opposite. A *simpático* group will make you feel welcome from your first meeting and embrace you with open arms when you offer to become more involved.

3. There are people your age in leadership positions or with the potential for leadership. If you are a twenty-something in a group run by near retirees, for example, you might want to think twice about that group. Or you might want to realize that new blood is going to be needed soon and decide to wait around for your chance to take control.

4. You have fun at meetings. Even board meetings can be fun if everyone is focused on the cause and trying to make things happen. At meetings like that, ideas arise fast and furiously and the leadership knows how to separate the good ones from the bad while keeping the meeting on track. You also should enjoy yourself at any events or volunteer opportunities the group offers. Otherwise, you'll find yourself avoiding the meetings even if you could meet powerful people there. Who wants to meet powerful bores?

Snobby people aren't going to become easier to deal with once you get to know them.

A NEW KIND OF FRIENDSHIP

Deep connecting, in my view, is nothing more than a formalized way of making and keeping friends. Some members of your network of connections will end up being social friends, and some will always remain only business contacts. But effective connecting has a lot more elements of friendship than most of us realize. If you want your connections to become deep connections, be sure to treat them the way you treat your very best friends.

- **Be considerate.** Take care of their needs before your own and always respond as quickly as you can.

- **Don't guilt-trip them.** Never take advantage of your connections or whine.

- **Be there.** Show that you care about them whether they are up or down. Listen.

- **Share yourself.** Relate on a personal level by asking them to share their life stories. Reveal pieces of your personal story that will help them understand you.

Friendship and networking really do go hand in hand. As Latinas, we are uniquely qualified to nurture warm friendships with our connections without taking advantage of them. Be a good friend to your connections and you'll grow the deep connections you need to succeed.

Does deep connecting work? Does the Pope know my friend Juanita Chacon? *Sí*, THE *Papa*. Chacon met him because one of her connections needed someone to be a greeter when the Pope visited Denver not long ago. She also has met people such as Jimmy Smits and Bill Clinton, as well as many, many people who became clients of her real estate business. How did she do it? By joining every group in sight when she moved to Denver about 15 years ago. "I joined the Hispanic Chamber of Commerce, the regular Chamber of Commerce, nonprofit boards," she told me. "I started chairing events, and now I'm a member of over twenty-five different boards! When I moved my contact information to my Palm last year, I found that I had easily over a thousand contacts. I'm now about two calls away from anyone I want to meet."

Chacon believes in keeping her contacts happy while helping herself and her causes: "Making connections between people is what I do best. I like to connect people from very different walks of life who would never otherwise meet, especially if it can help my nonprofit interests." That sentiment is what philosophers call enlightened self-interest. People we help *want* to help us. It's just a matter of getting to know them well enough to make the right offer of assistance. That's what deep connecting is all about.

People we help want *to help us.*

THE POWER OF MENTORING

I believe in the power of mentoring, and I'm talking about both being mentored and mentoring others. Both will move your career along nicely without a huge amount of effort, as surprising as that may be to higher-level women who feel they don't have the time or energy to mentor. They don't realize that mentoring takes deep connecting to another level, creating another web of people who want to help you succeed.

For many of us, our first experience with mentoring was when our mothers taught us to cook an old family recipe. In my case I remember *mi mamí* teaching me to make flour tortillas. She showed me how to mix flour and shortening, a pinch of salt, and baking soda in a bowl and then pour boiling water over it until it was doughy enough to make little *bolitas*. She'd roll them out with a rolling pin made out of a piece of pipe until they were smooth and clean and then put them on a hot griddle and watch them bubble up. Somehow, without measuring anything, she taught my hands to feel the right amount of flour and soda, the proper size of a pinch, just this much water, boiling hot. I still don't know exactly how much of any ingredient to use, but I make flour tortillas just the way *Mamí* did.

Such is the power of mentoring. You learn how things work without having to be told, just by observing and doing. Elisa D. Garcia was the first in her family to go to college and the very first even to think about becoming a lawyer. Despite that, she is now the highest-ranking Latina at Domino's Pizza, a billion-dollar company, serving as executive vice president and general counsel. But when she was starting out, she knew she needed someone to show her the ropes, and so she searched for a mentor. "I didn't ask anyone, 'Will you be my mentor?' because that might have scared people who didn't want the responsibility. Instead, I looked around for the person doing the most interesting work at my law firm and volunteered to help. Many times it's just a matter of linking up with something you'd be interested in doing anyway and offering to ease the burden of the person in charge. Then you just keep your eyes and ears open," says Garcia.

You learn how things work without having to be told, just by observing and doing.

Garcia now mentors three other women (two Latinas) in the same informal way. She selected the women herself—"I see who has the spark, who reminds me of me!"—because she is convinced that a mentoring relationship does more than anything else to lift promising employees to another, higher plane of success. Latinas especially benefit, she thinks. "Shadowing or spending time with Latina women who are successful opens up worlds for Latinas just starting out," she says.

Unfortunately, most people do not work for generous souls like Garcia. Catalyst, a nonprofit advocacy and research group that attempts to promote women in business, found in 2003 that Latinas believe that the lack of a mentor is the *numero uno* reason why they aren't advancing as fast as they'd like to at work. More than 300 ambitious Latinas participated in that study, in which Catalyst found that not having a mentor "makes it more difficult for Latinas to build successful relationships and harder to find the career supports that can make a difference when climbing the corporate ladder."

But even now, at the beginning of the twenty-first century, few companies in corporate America have recognized the importance of mentoring to the careers of talented people. Outside the largest companies, few formal mentoring programs exist. You're probably going to have to find a mentor or a series of mentors on your own. Fortunately, that's not as hard as it may seem. Almost everyone loves giving advice to someone who is eager to learn.

"Young Latinas especially need mentors," says Rosa Carrillo, a *mexicana* who came to the United States at age 10. "When everyone tells you you're crazy for wanting what you want, you need someone at your side to tell you differently." Carrillo is the president of Carrillo & Associates, a firm that advises companies such as GE and Nestle on leadership development. Mentoring, she says, is ideal for overcoming the emotional immaturity young people tend to bring to the workplace and toughens them up for the challenges ahead. But no one is ever too old to be able to learn something from a mentor who is further along in her (or his) career.

Sixty-four percent of Latinas say "My manager cares about my work satisfaction."

Creating Your Own Mentor

When I was young, I had to make my toys out of whatever I could find. Similarly, you can build a mentor "from scratch" (*"desde el principio"*) if you are motivated. The person you designate as your mentor doesn't have to call herself that or even be aware that you view her as one unless you want her to. You don't have to formalize anything. What you should be aiming for instead is a casual partnership that encourages you to ask for advice whenever you need it. If you snag the interest of someone relatively high in the company, it is also possible to create a mentor who will show you the inside track to the "plum" assignments that can get you noticed—and promoted.

> *You can build a mentor "from scratch"* ("desde el principio") *if you are motivated.*

Here's how you can build your own cuddly Frankenmentor, a person with all the advice and connections you need to become a bigger fish in your pond.

1. **Try a little admiration.** People have become my informal mentees simply by coming up to me after a speech or presentation and engaging me in conversation. They often tell me that something I've said has touched or inspired them. Then the good ones usually tell me how my words relate to their lives and how they'll apply them. Of course, I don't invite everyone who approaches me into a mentor relationship, but those who demonstrate a high level of ambition usually are invited to contact me again if they ask permission to do so. Most high-ranking people have healthy egos that respond to *sincere*

admiration. (Don't try this if you'll have trouble believing your own flattering words. Phony *adulación* gets you nowhere.)

2. **Seek specific knowledge.** "Tell me *everything* about . . ." is a heart-failure-inducing phrase to busy businesspeople. Nurture a budding mentor relationship with concrete questions that are not likely to take too long to answer. Especially when you first begin a mentorship, the last thing you want to do is make your mentor think of you as a pain in the neck, *una latosa*. But most people are happy to answer specific questions about a body of knowledge they possess. *Por ejemplo*, one of my early mentors, Carlos Soto, an executive at Coors, taught me how to interpret and then write marketing plans over the course of our relationship.

The last thing you want to do is make your mentor think of you as a pain in the neck, una latosa.

---

3. **Look outside your group.** Although having another Latina as a mentor is inspiring, the perspective you get from someone totally outside your experience can move you along even faster on occasion. Emma Sepulveda, Ph.D., a *chilena* who became the first Latina full professor at the University of Nevada, credits an Anglo man with putting her on the path to high achievement. He was a college professor of hers who had lived in Latin America, and he constantly pushed her to get her doctorate in English literature and achieve all that she could. Why a white

man? "There was no other source of advice; all my professors were white men, and they were the ones with the power to help me." Look at who holds the keys to power in your work setting and set your sights on recruiting one of those individuals as your mentor.

4. **Let the relationship percolate.** Get to know your mentor before you start making requests, even a request to meet for lunch or golf. Exchange e-mails for a while. Be charming and even helpful if you can. Learn your prospective mentor's interests. And be very grateful for any help you get. New mentor relationships in particular are helped along when you report back any positive results you achieved by following your mentor's advice. Only when you are sure that your mentor will not feel imposed on should you suggest regular meetings . . . or golf games!

5. **Don't be afraid to let some relationships die.** Not all mentor relationships turn into long-term things. Some are quite short-term and task-oriented. Once you've learned what you wanted to know from these mentors, you should not feel guilty about "graduating" to another level of connection. Perhaps you'll establish a deep connection with them; perhaps you'll contact them again only if you run across something that reminds you of them.

You should not feel guilty about "graduating" to another level of connection.

6. **Relax and enjoy.** Always remember that powerful people are just people. They will not want to spend much time with someone who is overly eager or fawning. Either is too intense for busy people to cope with. Just be your most charming, assertive self and have a good time learning at the feet of a great woman or man. Your chosen mentor will soon be ready to make considerable room for your meetings and clear some paths for you.

Why You Should Mentor Too

No matter how far (or how little) you have advanced in your career, you should start making time to mentor others. Even the lowliest assistant can make a difference in the lives of others who haven't been on the job as long. Also, it is almost certain that those you advise will remember you for years afterward. They even may end up in a position to hire you or promote you some day.

You can always tell who the people are who could benefit from your mentorship. They are the ones who seem fascinated by what the company does but unsure how to proceed. Or they talk about how they would change this or that if they were in charge. People who need mentoring certainly aren't the first ones out the door at 5 p.m. They stay until the work is done and often look around for something else to do after they've finished their own work. And sometimes it's just a hungry

---

Hispanic women need to be assertive and independent. They have to overcome the mildness that is fostered by the encouragement of ladylike behavior at home.

Laura Armesto, *professor of English, Chatham College*

---

look in someone's eye that you recognize; you know what it's like to hunger for achievement.

To be a good mentor, you need the willingness to spend time. You need to let your "mentee" set the agenda and not rush her. Don't just spout advice as soon as you *think* you understand what your mentee needs to know. If the wisdom you give is not the *right* wisdom, it will be useless. Listen for a while, saying mostly nothing, while you assess the scope of your mentee's challenges. Only then make suggestions for her to think about. Your mentee may think she wants solutions to her problems, but she'll learn more if you simply point her in the right direction.

You should reveal as much of yourself as you comfortably can to your mentee. A good mentor-mentee relationship is built on self-revelation. Ask about her family and outside interests so that you can understand her in context. If you can, get out from behind your desk and take her someplace where you can both relax (the golf course?).

Finally, if you have the power, clear some obstacles for your mentee in your organization. If she has proved her worthiness to you, introduce her to people she needs to know. Recommend her for a high-visibility project. Talk her up. Doing that will confer on you one of the great side benefits of mentoring: You will get the reputation of being a reliable nurturer of future talent, which is not a bad reputation to have in any workplace. Also, you get the warm fuzzies of a deed well done.

6
How *Mujeres* Can Win

*E*quality on the job is a fine thing, especially when it comes to pay. However, when it comes to the ways men and women struggle to reach the top, absolute equality is never gonna happen. Why? Simple. Most men and most women approach the "game" in radically different ways. Just look around if you don't believe me. Take the issue of personal success: Men tend to want to win at any cost, and so they are naturally more ruthless than women in trying to get what they want. Women, on the other hand, tend to value relationships at work more than winning every time, and so they put a premium on being a part of a successful team.

A 2003 study confirms what we already know intuitively. Northwestern University psychology professor Alice Eagly discovered that women tend to manage through "transformational" leadership. Transformational leaders are those who see themselves as role models, consciously encourage subordinates, and applaud creativity. In contrast, men tend to be "transactional" leaders who use rewards and punishments to change employees' perceptions of their own self-interest. Of course, not all women and not all men behave this way, but these generalities work enough of the time that it is useful to explore how women can navigate toward success in what is essentially still a man's world. (Hint: It's not by imitating the men.) In most workplaces, the glass ceiling is still hard and nearly impenetrable, and men still make almost all the rules. But resourceful *mujeres* can use those rules to win on their own terms in a whole *nuevo* game of office politics.

"PLAYING" WITH MEN'S RULES

The most important thing to remember as you aim for the top is that office politics really is a game. That shouldn't be surprising to anyone, seeing how important sports and competition are to a lot of men. Games like *fútbol*—and office politics—have easily understood rules, positions, fouls, and scores. They almost always have clear winners and losers. Your standing is clear to everyone: Your status as a winning guy typically is enhanced among your male peers if you support the winning side and wounded if you do not. Women, even if they are sports fans, tend not to get so invested in these contests—or in office politics. Most of us don't see the point of testing and retesting our "position" in the hierarchy to see who's up and who's down. Our reluctance to do that, however, can be used to our advantage. By not becoming invested in the office politics game, we can step outside it, observe its interactions and rules, and then play them to our advantage. Office politics also can "play" for us in another sense: We sometimes can even have fun with it. I know I've gotten a lot of *risas* out of it.

> *Office politics also can "play" for us in another sense: We sometimes can even have fun with it.*

Here are some of the things I've found work best in beating the guys at their own game. Call it being pushy in a nice way, which is the most effective way for a woman to win at office politics, *en mi opinión*.

Get Close to Power

This is actually funny to watch when men do it. When I was the station manager of Denver Univision, whenever the general manager or the president of the network visited, the men always tried to be seen with him. When we had a meeting of managers, you could expect a whole lot of jockeying among the *hombres* to position themselves near the top guy. Women as a whole don't seem to take part in this or even notice it to any great extent. But I've discovered that this is a reason why many top bosses don't see their female employees as being aggressive enough to be promoted into their ranks. Once I figured this out, I decided to do something about it.

Whenever I was going into an important meeting with a higher-up, I would always position myself somewhere outside the meeting room to welcome him or her. A warm greeting and a little small talk always turned the boss's attention toward me and made it seem natural that I would sit near him or her after we entered the room together. This maneuver creates respect for you among your bosses because you've gone out of your way to make them feel comfortable. It also almost subconsciously sends a message to your peers and subordinates that you are an up-and-comer. But far from being perceived as gamesmanship (although it is), a move like this typically is interpreted as graciousness on your part.

Getting close to power can be accomplished easily with another thing Latinas do naturally: offering to help. No, not by getting his coffee. "*Mami* didn't bring me up to be your maid," I've been known to tell guys who asked me to bring them *café*. The trick, as it has been so often in my experience, is to be observant. Listen closely and watch the people to whom you want to get close. Which projects are dear to their hearts? What needs do they complain about that don't seem to get met? One woman I know listened to her boss go on and on about how his salespeople were dropping the ball with customers, not following up on requests and closing the sales. She had a customized computer system created for the sales team that made follow-ups painless—and became a hero to her boss.

> *Listen closely and watch the people you want to get close to. Which projects are dear to their hearts?*

The point is that whatever you can figure out to get yourself noticed in a positive way by those in power can be an easy and reliable approach to getting close to power. Jockeying for chairs in a conference room may be the guys' way, but you can be much more sophisticated about the whole thing. You see now how this game can be played from a female perspective?

Give as Good as You Get

Many times high-level players in the office politics game (even other women) will attempt to insult you subtly or stab you in the back. The insults are easy to deal with if you always keep your sense of humor. You can use "verbal horseplay" to refuse to take an insult seriously even if it's meant that way. If you can turn it into a joke, the insulter won't have a leg to stand on! Suppose, though, that you're not fast on your feet in these situations or feel that such joking would diminish your authority. You need to get over that attitude in a hurry. Men tend to do this to new people in a workplace almost as an initiation ritual. If you let them walk on you in the beginning, it will never stop. Practice the eye roll and the "oh-come-off-it" put-down that you use to fend off jerks who hit on you after work. It works here too.

> *Practice the eye roll and the "oh-come-off-it" put-down that you use to fend off jerks who hit on you after work.*

Coworkers who are trying to stab you in the back require a more subtle response. Direct confrontation seldom works because backstabbing is easy to deny. "Who, me? I would never do that to her!" is the simplest dodge when a coworker is suspected of doing you wrong. Besides, you don't want to earn a reputation for being a tattletale. Instead, you need to rise to these challenges in a way that encourages people to take your side. The way to do that is to drop gentle hints about what's wrong, without naming names if you can, into the ears of people who can help. It can be as simple as saying, "I didn't know we were supposed to do this that way," referring to the methods of the person you suspect of sabotaging you. Eventually, your hints should alert the right people to the situation without your making a big scene. Of course, if nothing changes, you are also being sent a message: It's time to find another *empleo*.

Show a Little Machisma

Some of the "boys" will try to trip you up every time you attempt to move ahead. In those cases you need to respond to *machismo* with a little *machisma* of your own. You don't need to act like a man to be *machista*, though. You simply have to rise to the challenges with which you are faced. If you have a boss who "picks on you" or belittles you, don't even think about not responding. Men intend and interpret criticism to be helpful whether they are the target or the source of it. Don't take it personally or as an attack. Many of these bosses are trying to help you develop a thicker skin or a better project in their own misguided way. Stand up to them. Call them on it if you feel they are wrong. A man would; he would be expected to by the other men.

> *You need to respond to* machismo *with a little* machisma *of your own.*

Just do it in a friendly, noncomplaining way: "I see that you have some problems with my (whatever). When can we schedule a brainstorming session to discuss it? I'm interested in your suggestions." Even if you are not the least bit interested in his suggestions, showing that you are operating in a spirit of give-and-take should lower the level of *machismo* a bit. After all, you essentially are saying that you agree that a critique may help, for the good of the team. You want to show that you are strong enough, as good as anyone else you are playing the game with, and that you want to be the best player you can be for the "coach."

Don't Be Fouled Out by Dirty Tricks

Unfortunately, women who become good at the game of office politics often find that the fight is only beginning. Don't worry: This can be the most amusing part of the game. You'll know you're getting close to the goal line if you find yourself on the receiving end of any of these "slick" moves.

"Do You Mind?"

Be alert for this maneuver and turn off your natural Latina politeness. It's usually said by someone who wants the position near power that you've staked out for yourself. Yes, you do mind. Make a space for the requester, but one that's farther away from the power position than you are. This may take some fancy footwork, but that's something that we Latinas are good at, *no?*

Know when to turn off your natural Latina politeness.

"Can I Say Something?"

Often, when we're in the middle of a point or a presentation, this little question will pop up from somewhere. Nine times out of ten it comes from a man. Or an *hombre* will just start talking about his own point, interrupting you without permission. Men do this to each other all the time. If the boss does not intervene to shut the interrupter down, there is only one course of action that will work for you as a *mujer*. You can't shout the interrupter down because women's voices are not low-pitched enough to carry as far as men's do. Instead, you must keep talking in your normal tone of voice, paying no attention to the attempt to cut you off. Eventually it will become apparent to everyone in the room how professional you are and how rude the interrupter is. In almost every case that's enough to make someone else in the room request that you repeat what you just said so that everyone can hear it. And if that doesn't work, keep interrupting your interrupter firmly and loudly. (Learn to speak from the belly; a speech coach can teach you how.) Once again, you need to suppress your natural instincts for politeness and give as good as you get if you can't get your points across any other way. Trust me, everyone will respect you more if you cease being a doormat.

"¿Me Traes . . . ?"

It could be the latest prospectus, the Smith file, or *un café*. Whatever it is, if it's not a big inconvenience for us, our temptation is to fetch it and move on. Don't do that! This is a power play, pure and simple, and I always call them on it. "I didn't know we were married!" I'll say. Guys who do this, especially if they're Latino, remind me so much of my five brothers, and not in a good way. This is the kind of guy who has been trained by *mami* to have everything done for him. In fact, these men are kind of resentful when you don't anticipate their needs. They're the kind who'll leave a coffee cup beside the empty coffee maker and then be mad if they come back later and the coffee hasn't magically appeared. Your answer to these petty requests should almost always be, "I'm too busy right now." But for the worst offenders I just turn it around a few times as they pass my desk, and then they get the point: "Corazon, will you get me a cup of *café* as long as you're up anyway?"

"To Be Perfectly Honest with You . . ."

Watch out for this phrase and its variants (actually, in truth, everyone knows, etc.). Men tend to, um, stretch the truth more often in work situations than women do. This makes sense because preserving relationships, remember, is less important to them than winning personally. Precisely because relationships are important to us, we tend to minimize the untruths that we recognize in the interest of preserving the relationship. This is a bad idea: You must address even small factual inaccuracies immediately or you'll be setting yourself up for much bigger trouble down the road. It doesn't matter if the person doing the exaggerating is lower or higher than you are in the food chain. You want to establish the fact that truthfulness is important to you. But do it privately, at least when you first discover the problem. Don't make a public stink about it until you are sure that the offending party is not going to rectify his "error."

> *You must address even small factual inaccuracies immediately or you'll be setting yourself up for much bigger trouble down the road.*

"Oh, Baby, Honey, Dear..."

The last resort of the threatened *hombre* is his *machismo*. Comments on your desirability as a sex partner, your sexy body, and so on, should be seen for what they are: desperate ploys by insecure men to knock you out of contention for the top spots. It does not matter to these guys that such comments are illegal (in the United States). The *hombres* who say these things are certain you won't jeopardize your position in the company by fighting them in the executive suite or in court. You are much more likely to leave for greener pastures, which is exactly the outcome they are looking for. (You rarely hear such things from men who are secure in their power, only from those to whom you represent a credible threat to their own rise up the corporate ladder.)

I recommend that you respond in a way that's guaranteed to take the wind out of most *macho* guys', um, sails: Laugh and thank them. "What a great guy you are, Al. You know I'm (married, engaged, a nun—pick one). But it's so rewarding to know that I've still got it going on." Keep laughing and get others to laugh with you. Of course, if the harassment doesn't stop, you shouldn't ignore it. If he's doing it to you, he's probably doing it to others who may be less able to cope with it than you are. Report the incidents to the higher-ups but don't whine about them. Simply report matter-of-factly what you've observed about another employee's behavior that is damaging to morale and is getting in the way of productivity. Then continue to report it, without emotion, every time it happens. Then let's see who ends up leaving the company.

> *More than 470,000 Latinas now own businesses contributing $29 billion a year to the U.S. economy.*

PLAYING POLITICS FOR KEEPS: THE PROBLEM OF DISCRIMINATION

Sometimes no amount of humor or attitude will help you much. Evidence suggests you will face discrimination or an intolerably hostile work environment that blocks your progress to the top at some point in your career, and that's in spite of all the strides women and people of color have made in this country. *Por ejemplo*, Pastora San Juan Cafferty, a professor at the University of Chicago, serves on the board of directors of Kimberly-Clark Corporation, the makers of Kleenex and many other products. She was the first Latina ever to be elected to the board of a Fortune 1000 company (the nation's largest companies), achieving that in 1976. Today nineteen Latinas serve on the boards of those companies. Look at that again: Nineteen of 1,000 largest companies have a Latina on their boards. Twenty-five years later and we're up to 2 percent representation. *Ay!* Aren't we making great strides! (No, we are not. I'm not a board member of one of those companies and I certainly am qualified to be.) Even worse, the Hispanic

Association on Corporate Responsibility (HCAR) says that 35 industries in that fortunate 1,000 have *no* Hispanics at all (male or female) in *any* executive position.

Both Latinas and Latinos believe that discrimination is still a huge problem in general and in the workplace. According to the Pew Hispanic Center 2002 National Survey of Latinos, fully a third of the male and female respondents had personally experienced discrimination in the last five years because of their race or ethnicity. (Shockingly, 83 percent also reported that they believed that discrimination by Hispanics against other Hispanics was still a major problem. The reasons cited included disparities in income, education, language skills and even country of origin or ancestry.) Nearly half of those questioned reported "being treated with less respect than others" and "receiving poorer service than others" to have been the kind of unfair treatment they or someone in their families had experienced.

> *Both Latinas and Latinos believe that discrimination is still a huge problem in general and in the workplace.*

Still, things are definitely looking up from where we were when I started out, but only if you don't consider how far along we should be by now. In 2003 we had seven Latina members of the U.S. Congress. (That's only 1 percent of the total when we represent about 3 percent of the American population. We still have a ways to go. Anyone out there considering politics? You should.) Latinas are much more common everywhere now, but at the top levels of power in government, business, and even charitable organizations we are still very rare. Is that because of discrimination, or are there simply not enough of us yet with the qualifications to take the reins of power? Many believe it is the former: "We have a database of 2,000 Hispanics who are well-qualified to sit on corporate boards and assume executive positions," Omar Velarde-Wong of HCAR told the *Wall Street Journal* in 2003. "But you don't see demand coming from companies to recruit them."

Not to put too fine a point on it, many men in the business world would prefer that we not be there. They wish they could find a way to make us toddle off home to take care of our kids. When I started out, they tried to accomplish that by asking us in interviews what kind of birth control we used and how we could manage to take care of our kids if they were kind enough to offer us a job. But since overt discrimination like that is no longer legal, some men stop at nothing to make us feel like "interlopers." In her research for *Secrets of Six-Figure Women* Barbara Slanny ran across dozens of horror stories about men who belittled executive women by one means or another. One woman reported that an executive had relieved himself in front of her. Another was left shaking with anger after fellow executives left her behind when their corporate jet took off for home—with her purse and other belongings aboard.

Attorney Berta Hernández-Truyol, a law professor at the University of Florida, believes that discrimination has not gone away, it simply has gone underground: "Discrimination is not that easy to uncover at work. You may just have the feeling that you are being prevented from advancement or being subjected to uncomfortable working conditions." And that's not something you can fight in court, even if the law didn't make it exceptionally difficult for Latinas especially to prove. How do the federal antidiscrimination laws make it hard? They say that you may sue for racial discrimination *or* sexual discrimination but not both. So what is a woman of color to do?

Hernández-Truyol suggests that if things get bad, you should call on the company ombudsman, if such a thing exists, or ask the company to hire a professional mediator. These are good suggestions when you have an intractable situation, but you don't want to come across as weak or whiny, which you may if you "tattle" in this way. I think that in most cases you can still cut subtle discrimination off at the pass by being ultra-professional and having a sense of humor at all times. (That executive who piddled in front of his coworker, in other words, deserved a good razzing.) Don't get mad; get cracking. You can earn respect by always having good ideas, doing your homework to back them up, and always being emotionally on an even keel even if it kills you. Don't be a good Latina, respectful in all situations, no matter how demeaning. Demand respect through good work and you will get it. Then you'll find that your actions will do a lot of your public relations (and your office politics) for you.

◆

HELPFUL ORGANIZATIONS

- **The Feminist Majority Foundation**

For a list of professional women's networking organizations, go to http://www.feminist.org/gateway/womenorg.html.

- **Hispanic Women in Leadership**

An organization providing scholarships, training opportunities, and role models for Latinas on the rise. Go to www.hwil.org.

- **International Links for Networking Women**

For women's organizations outside the United States. Go to www.advancingwomen.com/intlinks.html.

- **Mujeres de Empresa**

(In Spanish.) Events, business opportunities, and networking for businesswomen, primarily in relation to Central and South America. Go to www.mujeresdeempresa.com.

- **National Hispana Leadership Institute**

A Washington, D.C., area leadership training institute that trains Latinas of all ages to assume power. Its mission is to "develop Hispanas as ethical leaders." Go to www.nhli.org.

- **National Society of Hispanic MBAs**

If you have an MBA, want to find an MBA to hire, or just want to find out if the degree will help you advance, visit nshmba.org.

- **SBA Online Women's Business Center**

Find information about starting a business, getting funding, and finding a Women's Business Development Center near you. Go to www.onlinewbc.gov.

- **U.S. Hispanic Chamber of Commerce**

An organization designed to focus the power of Hispanic business leaders and represent their interests in the public and private sectors. Many cities have strong chapters of the USHCC, with outstanding networking opportunities. Find your local chapter at www.ushcc.com/chamberdirectory.htm.

- **U.S. Hispanic Leadership Institute**

An organization dedicated to empowering minorities and maximizing participation in the electoral process. Go to www.ushli.org.

THE POWER OF POSITIVE POLITICS

Claro, not all men are snakes when it comes to office politics. You and I both know men who are perfect gentlemen in all their dealings with women at work. They would no more play dirty tricks on us than they would wear mismatched shoes to work. Of course, some of these guys are simply very good at hiding the games they are playing; they're the dangerous ones, and you have to be constantly on the alert for people (men and women) who try to build themselves up by pulling you down.

But let's give the guys the benefit of the doubt for a few minutes. What can we as women learn about winning at office politics from men who are doing it the right way? By "the right way," I mean office politics that lets you shine without detracting from anyone else. Call it *the power of positive politics.* That's the kind of office politics that allows you to forge smoothly ahead, creating alliances, allies, and "rabbis" who will do everything in their power to help you rise to the top. And it's based on something most of us Latinas are fantastically good at: making people want to be around us.

Almost two-thirds of Hispanic women work (55.9 percent in 1999, projected to grow to 57.9 percent in 2008).

Linda Dominguez, a *puertorriqueña* executive coach in California and the author of *How to Shine at Work,* says that women first of all should not think of politics as an all or nothing proposition: "Some people say you've got to get into office politics wholeheartedly or avoid it completely. Both are wrong." She suggests that instead women can win at office politics by making sure their focus is on "what is right for the organization rather than what is right for any one individual, even if that individual is yourself." She advises you to be "*a beacon*," demonstrating through words and actions that you are interested only in what's best for the company. With that kind of attitude, political games may still go on around you, but you will have put yourself above them. It also will make the "gamesmen" look a little petty next to your dedication to getting the job done.

If you find it difficult to remold your attitudes in this way, and it may be especially challenging if you work in a politically toxic workplace, Dominguez advises using an executive coach to help you develop personal strategies: "A coach can help you identify gaps between where you are and where you want to be." (Find a coach at www.findacoach.com.) Coaches generally charge $100 and up for their services but should be willing to give you an initial consultation for free. It could be money extremely well spent. A coach can help you when your *amigas* are as clueless about how to play office politics as you may be. However, if you know someone who is really terrific at getting along with everyone at work and is moving ahead with apparent ease, invite her to lunch and ask her advice about your particular situation. You may be surprised how willing to help she is—especially if you pick up the check.

Another way to avoid the downside of office politics is to monitor and model the ethical behavior of the successful men around you. or, if you see or are the target of unethical behavior, profit from it by figuring out how to accomplish the same thing ethically. Remember my suggestion that you "accidentally" meet your boss in the corridor before a meeting? It's the solution I came up with after observing the guys jockeying for position and trying to shove me aside (verbally and literally) once the meeting has started. In a sense I'm telling you to steal from them. Copy a successful tactic in your own words and your own style, turning it from a possibly dirty trick into an ethical business practice.

You also can steal a couple of other techniques that guys use successfully all the time: acting fearless and never admitting to being wrong. These are actually two sides of the same coin. Many successful men call it putting on their "game face." As boys they're taught that if the other team ever suspects they're not ready for a sporting event, they'll get killed on the field, and so they learn to hide their emotions behind a wall of confidence. Sometimes that confidence is real; sometimes it's entirely faked. But it looks the same to observers—an easy assurance that the game's in the bag. They bring that same confident look to the business arena even if they are shaking in their *zapatos*. They never let anyone see them sweat.

Mujeres, en cambio, often exude an air of tentativeness if they are unsure of themselves in any way. Will a client ask for a figure I can't give him? Do I know enough about my subject? Are my conclusions adequately supported? Any and all of these questions are swirling around in the heads of many of the guys around you too, but you'll never see the successful ones appear to be bothered by that. They do what you should do: prepare as well as they can for any situation and then wing it! And whatever you do, don't admit that you are wrong or unprepared. *Por ejemplo,* if asked by a client for a figure you don't have, never say, "I don't know." Of course you could admit you don't have the information and offer to get back to her. That's what conventional business wisdom suggests. But a stronger, more positive response is to call on your business experience and intuition and just name a figure. Then, when you get back to your office, find or recalculate the figure as soon as possible. If you were "off," call and say that you went over the figures again and now have a "more accurate" estimate. You are telling the truth: You made an estimate that was based on your knowledge at the time, and it wasn't quite right. This is not a problem for either your client or yourself. You've kept everything on a positive note, passed along accurate information in a timely manner, and come across as prepared and professional. And you've moved the project forward. What could be "wrong" with that? It is all a matter of being light on your feet and always appearing to be in control, even when you don't feel that way.

Don't admit that you are wrong or unprepared.

Having a light touch also helps when you're trying to negotiate office relationships. Successful men often accuse ambitious women of being too serious and too earnest. I admit that early in my career I sometimes took things so seriously that I was almost in tears. Crying, though, is about the worst thing you can do at work. Smile instead. When things get rough, think about how funny the story will sound when you tell your *amigas* about it. *Mira*, it's just work! What does it mean in the overall scheme of things if Roger interrupted you for the fourteenth time today? Everybody knows what a pill Roger is, so, call him on it with a laugh in your voice. "There goes old Roger again, enjoying the sound of his own voice." Pretty soon everybody will be on your side instead of Roger's. And if you find yourself still terribly upset about the politics at your workplace, find a new job or get some interests outside of work so that what happens on the job will lose a little of its importance. Work troubles tend to look awfully puny when you're feeding hungry children at a shelter or teaching an immigrant to read English. When your priorities are straight, you can enjoy the humor that's always present in office politics as long as you can just step back far enough to see it. Go on a snake patrol today—look for examples of coworkers behaving childishly—and make people wonder what you're laughing at.

> Mira, *it's just work!*

THE MANAGER AS *MADRE*

If you aren't a manager already, you will be one day soon. To be an effective boss you must make a choice that I believe is critical: You must choose your management style. As Latinas, most of us are culturally unsuited for the authoritarian style of "the boss who must be obeyed." This is not a bad thing. We would rather develop the relationship-oriented, team-centered style that's been popularized as "participative management." But I recommend that you take that general style one step further. I did, and I was able to build teams of employees who were both loyal and relatively stress-free. Let's call it the "good mother" management style. I don't mean the kind of mother who holds your hand and kisses your ouchies. Hardly. I'm thinking of the kind of mother who teaches you everything you need to know, creates a safe environment in which you can learn, and then boots you out of the nest to soar on your own.

> *As Latinas, most of us are culturally unsuited for the authoritarian style of "the boss who must be obeyed." This is not a bad thing.*

It is a style that came very naturally to me. I didn't have any experience being a boss when I first became one, and so I applied to the workplace lessons I learned bringing up my kids. And did my kids ever teach me about management!

A Good Boss Teaches Independence

For me, a major pillar of my good mother style is to let the "kids" take on the world in their own ways. If that means forming close-knit teams to solve problems, that's what a good mother encourages. If it means going off to play cops and robbers with a crew of adventurers, that's okay too. And if an artistic type wants to be left alone to create, the good mother tries to make that happen too. She lets these interactions happen on their own, intervening only when someone is left out intentionally or play becomes hurtful.

Further, I try very hard never to second-guess people who have good reasons for doing what they are doing even if I disagree. You have to let your employees fall off their bikes from time to time or you'll be baby-sitting all the time. In other words, micromanaging and authoritarianism rarely work, especially in the modern workplace of independently minded young people. You have to let all your employees "grow up" and become independent of you. The key when you're delegating is to set deadlines for decisions and action and then hold people accountable for those deadlines. If you don't, the company will suffer because you'll have a timid and dependent staff. Just like a good mother, you put the training wheels on when they need them, take them off when they're ready, and then watch your "kids" disappear from sight, knowing they'll be okay because you've taught them well.

A Good Boss Makes People Feel Especial

The trick is to instill that feeling in both kids and employees. I always try to pick out something that each one does (kids and employees) particularly well on a regular basis and praise it. You can't be praising all the time for praising's sake, though, because that would devalue the worth of your compliments. Taking the time to notice something particularly well done, however, works wonders. I always tried to make employees feel better about themselves, especially if they were so battered on their last jobs that they were convinced they were lucky to have a job at all.

Encouragement is a big part of my style of management. Catch them doing something right. You'll be surprised how much it makes people walk on air—and work their hardest to please you again. Be careful about personal comments, though, unless you have a particularly close or casual relationship with your employees. Otherwise, compliments about clothes, hair, or lifestyle choices can cause them to think, "Why is she all up in my business? What does she want?" Instead of fostering closer relations, that kind of thing can breed suspicion and hostility. It's just like when you quiz your teenagers about school, friends, and life. You're just curious; you want to be a part of their lives. But you know (if you've had the pleasure of parenting teens) that they tend to interpret it as prying. There is no better way to turn a teenager—and many employees— away from you.

A Good Boss Understands That You Have a Life Outside Work

I had one boss who always scheduled mandatory meetings on Friday afternoon or Monday morning so that no one could take a long weekend. He was just trying to prove who was boss. In that way he was like the parent who forbids a kid to go on a school camping trip because "that's the weekend we have to clean the garage." Almost any weekend would be fine for such a task, but forbidding a fun activity shows who is in control of the family. Good mothers and good bosses never engage in such power trips, although sometimes the urge can be overwhelming. To me such behavior reeks of disrespect for employees' desire to control their own lives. Control freaks are hurt in another way too: No one who is managed by such a person will ever speak up in time to correct a mistake. They'd rather see the boss fall flat on his or her face.

A Good Boss Rarely Surprises People

Catching people by surprise is a management technique that is favored by bad managers (and bad parents). If they can catch you doing something wrong—or even looking guilty—they can keep you off balance. It's hard to say exactly why they do it, but it seems to enable such managers to feel superior to the people they manage. There is also the element of "I know they must be doing something wrong; I just haven't caught them at it yet." You might as well rent a neon sign flashing "I don't trust my employees" when you install (or allow to be installed) keystroke-monitoring equipment or surveillance cameras. Same thing if you ambush them in meetings with information that changes the conclusions they are about to draw or undercuts a presentation they are making. A good mother teaches her children the right things to do and then trusts them enough not to spy on them or sabotage them unless there is solid evidence that all is not well. Even then, she takes them aside and talks about the matter. She does not make a public spectacle of suspected wrongdoing just to put the fear of God into the other kids.

A Good Boss Does Not Break Promises

Remember what happened when you promised your kids they could have ice cream if they were good on a shopping trip? What happened if you suddenly remembered you had to stop by your *mami's* house and had to cancel the trip to the Dairy Queen? The good behavior you were enjoying went all to hell, didn't it? Exactly the same thing happens in companies all the time. Employees structure their behavior on the basis of what you've told them about reward systems, future plans, and likely promotions. Morale takes a major blow to the head if you then have to say, "Corporate wouldn't let me do what I promised you we were going to do." You can lose a lot of good people as a result of blown promises, and the people who are left behind are unlikely to trust you deeply ever again. The result is half-assed effort and rampant cynicism about the company—and about you. Who can blame them? After all, you promised them ice cream and they got an afternoon at Tia Marta's.

Make sure that what you promise is absolutely the truth, so help you Dios.

The solution? Make sure that what you promise employees (and kids) is absolutely the truth, so help you *Dios*. A lot of us—me included—tend to make vague promises we haven't thought through completely. We don't take them seriously, but our listeners do. If you want to talk about such possibilities, never let them be construed as firm promises. Instead of saying, "You'll all get bonuses if sales reach X," say instead that you're going to try your damnedest to get bonuses for the staff and will keep them posted on your progress. That probably won't boost sales (or good behavior) in the short run as much as a false promise would, but good mothers know that outstanding performance over time is what really counts.

A Good Boss Helps Employees Get Along

Some mothers and many bosses insist on breaking up conflicts by asserting their authority: "Stop that right now or go to your room!" Of course, although there are rarely pinch fights in the workplace, conflict in all its forms certainly can make its presence felt. In a work situation it is much more likely to break out in the form of backstabbing and other underhanded power plays. Or it can be as simple as one person being set on one plan or idea and someone else being set on another one. How do you come to an agreement? How do you enforce a compromise? Managers can stop any conflict by sheer force of will, but all that is likely to do is drive such conflicts underground, where they become even harder to deal with and more destructive. A better solution, I think, is one that worked well with my children and is still keeping the peace when my little grandbabies come to visit. One of my grandchildren readily shares his toys, but the other one doesn't, at least without prompting. When Mary, the nonsharer, has her cousin Nicholas visiting at her house and doesn't want to share, I ask her to remember how Nicholas shared his toys the last time Mary visited his home. That causes a light to go on even in this little girl's brain.

You can treat your employees the same way: like adults who respond to logical argument rather than children who need a time-out. Ask them to figure out between themselves what the real source of the conflict is and what would resolve the differences between them. After they've uncovered the source of the conflict, take yourself totally out of the picture in terms of imposing a solution. Just throw them into a conference room and don't let them out until they can play nice! Forcing people to talk it out usually results in a workable solution. If the conflict is severe and the combatants can't make any headway on their own, you should step in and help them reach a compromise everyone can live with. But most conflicts can be resolved with a little application of logic, discussion, and the conviction of a good boss that things can be worked out.

A Good Boss Makes Employees Feel Secure

Children who are fearful tend to develop a set of repetitive behaviors that minimize their chances of getting in trouble. Instinctively, they want to drop off the radar and not be noticed by the adults in their lives who could make life even harder for them. Forget creativity and active play. These kids sit in the corner, playing quietly, hoping no one will notice them. Employees who are fearful act in much the same way. They do not want to be the nails that stick up when the next hammer comes along. Creative ideas and approaches dry up when your employees depend on tried and true methods for getting through the day.

> *This is a time to kick up your instincts as a* mujer *and mother.*

The fearful atmosphere might not even be your fault. In times of corporate upheaval and layoffs—even at other companies—employees can lose their sense that good performance on the job makes a difference. It is vitally important in this kind of atmosphere to avoid playing one "child" against another by making people fight for rewards. This is the worst time to try to keep employees on their toes by reminding them that they easily could lose their "allowances": jobs, commissions, and/or bonuses. Instead, this is a time to kick up your instincts as a *mujer* and mother. You must be exquisitely attuned to the way your actions will be perceived in terms of fairness and explain apparent discrepancies carefully. You also must continue to share, share, share when it comes to information. At least 95 percent of what you know about the company and its workings can be passed on to your employees. And if they know you are doing all you can to keep them informed, the fear level will dissipate so that creativity can flourish again. All that people expect from parents and bosses is the truth. Treat them like grown-ups, in other words. Any good mother knows that kids love that.

7

La Rica "Look": Acting the Part

You probably are a great judge of who is likely to succeed in your workplace. You can look around at work and tell precisely who is at the top, who is almost certainly headed for better things, and who will be stuck at the bottom forever. Most women, in fact, know instinctively what success looks like, but far fewer women consistently mold their personal image to smooth their rise up the corporate ladder.

In a very real sense creating a business *imagen* that helps you get ahead is like acting. At every stage of your career you can make your clothes, hair, makeup, and presence say precisely what you want at work. Without ever having to say "I'm ambitious and looking for an opportunity," you can convey that message solely through the way you look. By contrast, if you aren't paying close enough attention, you can shout a message completely different from the one you intend. Remember the micro-miniskirts Ally McBeal used to wear? Those thigh-high outfits certainly didn't shout, "I want to be a partner in this firm!" The same thing goes for many of the beautiful clothes the girls wore on *Sex in the City*. Sure, they had the sexy, funky part down cold, but does anyone believe that those women wanted to get ahead at work? And don't get me started on what the women in the *telenovelas* are saying with their outfits cut up to here and down to there!

Without ever having to say "I'm ambitious and looking for an opportunity," you can convey that message solely through the way you look.

I want to let you in on some ways to make sure your image is doing its best for you on the job. That process begins with an examination of exactly who will be in the "audience" when you make your next star turn on the business stage.

PLAYING TO YOUR AUDIENCE

Like an actress, you should consider your business image to be something you put on, like a costume. Your image is something that you can create to match the message you wish to convey in any business situation. When you are attempting to establish authority, *por ejemplo*, you may want to put on the most expensive tailored suit you can afford, one that doesn't look a bit mannish. However, when I need to build a cooperative team effort, I often wear slacks and sweater sets, perhaps with a pastel cardigan casually draped over my shoulders. When my primary message is "I'm creative and exciting," I apply funky touches like a chunky colorful necklace or a fringed scarf. Whatever I wear, though, I'm exquisitely aware of the impression it is going to make on observers and try to make certain that impression matches the image I need to convey. That is, I play to the audience.

> *Your image is something that you can create to match the message you wish to convey in any business situation.*

How do you play to an audience in the workplace? You certainly don't have to adopt some kind of uniform. Every workplace is different, and you'll need to adapt your image to fit it. But there are a few underlying principles that will help you project the *imagen* that will make the best impression on your most important audiences.

1. **Remember where you want to go.** By now you have a clearer idea of where you want your career path to lead you. How do women dress, talk, and carry themselves at that level? What do you want to change about your own presentation to project an image that is more like theirs?

2. **Copy, but not slavishly.** You want to make yourself fit in with powerful women as much as possible without being obvious about it. Do all the women at the level you aspire to wear St. John suits? If you are an assistant now, it will look odd if you suddenly start wearing them too. (For one thing, people may wonder where you are getting the money.) But if powerful women all look tailored and polished, that is the image you should project even if you never wear a suit. A workplace where the powerful dress more creatively will inspire you to project a different image. The key is to figure out the *image style* your role models have adopted. Whether it is tailored, creative, funky, fashionable,

casual, or something else, you will look much more like a *mujer con ambición* if you copy that style.

3. **Pick an image mentor.** To refine your image, select one role model in your workplace or in the industry you aspire to enter. Pick a woman you admire both for her ideas and for her ability to draw favorable attention to herself. Let this woman be your image mentor. She doesn't have to know that she's playing that role for you. Observe how she moves, how she dresses, and her use of makeup. Listen to her use of language when she speaks and take note of how she captures and holds your attention. If possible, obtain photos of her and copies of her speeches. Try to isolate the kind of image she projects and the way she does it. What elements of her style could you incorporate into your own?

4. **Consider your meetings.** As you dress each morning, select your outfit on the basis of the meeting that will have the most impact on your progress at work. Perhaps that will be a team meeting you are leading. Dressing too formally for that gathering might get in the way of building a solid team. Meeting with clients? You need to dress in the same image style they use so that they'll feel comfortable. Dressing in layers can make it possible to adapt your image for a variety of audiences, but take along a costume change on certain days if you think you're going to need one. Creating an appropriate image is that important. (Putting on more or removing some makeup also can allow you to flex your image, as can adapting your language style to be closer to that of your listeners.)

Mujeres who are just starting out in the business world can apply these principles too. Susan Stewart, a *colombiana-americana* in her twenties, found that she could get more work as an actress when she wore tiny miniskirts to auditions even though she ordinarily wears slacks in her work as a New York publicist. She often takes a change of clothes with her on the subway if there's an audition scheduled. "The lesson I learned is to dress for the situation," she says. Don't get the idea, though, that Susan and I are saying you need to be something that you are not or wear things that are not "you." You must keep it real in order not to look like a phony. I am only advising that you need to be aware at all times of what your image is saying in any context. In a sense, you are being yourself "*plus*."

Susan notes that she never ties herself in knots or wears clothes she feel constricted in while projecting a calculated message. "I want to be comfortable," she says, "because if I'm comfortable, I can project an image of confidence." Yet she does not believe in taking the idea of comfort too far. "You'll get a much better deal in this world if you don't look too schlumpy—or too sexy. Even if I'm just running an errand like getting the car serviced, I'll put on a little makeup and maybe a skirt. You just get better treatment that way."

Yes, you will. You will get better treatment by the world at large if your image conveys the message that you expect to be valued. Women who project an image of "I don't care" or "I'm very sexy" can expect to be treated in the way that message demands. Unfortunately, too few of us are adequately aware of the messages we are conveying. I can't tell you the number of employees I've had to take aside and talk to about the images they were projecting at work. Many of those *mujeres* were ambitious to the max, but most of them were completely unaware that their outside appearance did not match their vision of themselves. They simply copied the images they saw in magazines, in movie stars or—¡*Dios mío!*—in *novelas*. Even at a Spanish-language television station nobody who wanted to get ahead dressed like that.

You will get better treatment by the world at large if your image conveys the message that you expect to be valued.

Here's the problem: We Latinas want to look good at all times, and that can get us in trouble. "Looking good" has many definitions, depending on the situation we are facing. *Claro*, what works in the clubs doesn't work at work, but you'd be surprised how many of my Latina sisters don't know that. We even tend to like our bodies too much, as the young *chica* Ana demonstrates in the movie *Real Women Have Curves*. Perhaps it shouldn't surprise us that we attract *machismo* treatment when we are showing too much skin, too much cleavage, too much—all right, I'll say it—butt. But that doesn't mean that we have to wear boring suits or conservative church-lady clothes to work in order to get ahead. Far from it. In its own way, that kind of "dressing for success" pigeonholes us just as effectively as does wearing clothes that are too sexy. It says that we have no imagination, no style, no flair. What we need to do is bring together elements of image that convey that we are bright and imaginative as well as ambitious and serious. As Latinas, we have the art in our souls to bring off that combination exceedingly well. So why don't we always do that at work? In my personal experience, it's because we have so many ideas about what would look great that we get lost in the possibilities.

> *Claro, what works in the clubs doesn't work at work, but you'd be surprised how many of my Latina sisters don't know that.*

My solution, besides always being aware of the image style of my audience in each situation, is to focus on what I have decided to call "*la rica* look," the rich look. I decided early on, even before I could afford it, that I would do everything I could to look like I had money. That, I figured, would help money find its way to me. (And it worked, didn't it?)

HOW TO ACHIEVE THE RICH LOOK

You can't trust the fashion magazines, the stores, or the designers to help you "dress rich." According to most of them, you'll do just fine at work in peasant blouses, low-cut pants, mules, or a flowery, flouncy miniskirt. Don't believe them. Susan Bixler, author of *Five Steps to Professional Presence: How to Project Confidence, Competence and Credibility at Work*, says that to do that is to risk sending out the wrong message entirely: "If a working woman wants the words 'credible, appropriate and professional' used about her, she dresses and acts one way. If it is 'sexy, fun and outrageous,' she dresses another way. When we buy into diminishing our credibility, we're part of the problem and not the solution." Exactly. Unless you work in fashion retailing, advertising, or some other creative field, *la rica* look is a better choice. Here's how to achieve it even if you don't have a huge budget. Spending huge amounts of money is not necessary if you make careful choices about your clothes, hair, makeup, accessories, and "presence."

> *Unless you work in fashion retailing, advertising, or some other creative field,* la rica *look is a better choice.*

Project "Presence" with a Confident Body Image

Ninety-nine percent of us do not have perfect figures. (And I'm real mad at that 1 percent, *chica*.) But even the most imperfect woman can electrify a room if she carries her figure with confidence and style. That means always standing up straight and gliding effortlessly as you move instead of clumping around. (You do sometimes, don't you?.) Gliding isn't hard once you know that it's just a matter of putting one foot directly in front of the other as you walk. But that's not a natural way of walking for most women, and it may take some effort to remember to glide every time. If you don't, though, avoid being videotaped from the back! (Waddle, waddle.) As for standing up straight, that also can be harder than it seems, especially if you've been casual about it up to now. When we sit slumped at our desks or TVs, our chest muscles actually contract, making it more difficult to stand straight even if we want to. If you can't tell, ask a friend to tell you if you walk or sit slumped over. Even if her mouth says *"claro que no,"* her eyes will tell you the truth.

The best remedy for posture that is poor or even becoming poor is exercise, ideally with a personal trainer, at least until you know some exercises that will help you straighten up. Wearing flatter shoes also can help you straighten up and glide more easily. There's nothing like a three-inch heel to give you a swayback like *una vaca*!

A confident body image also comes from accepting the shape you're in, whatever that is. Sure, you want to diet and exercise as needed to get to your ideal weight, but in the meantime love what you've got. That means not complaining to anyone about your weight or shape, particularly at work. And it means *buying clothes that fit.* So many *mujeres* want to be a size 10 or 8 or 4 that they'll squeeze into their ideal size even though it's just a meaningless number. The result often is too-deep cleavage, stretched buttons, bunched-up sleeves, and wrinkly clothes. Clothes that fit don't fight you They drape your figure in attractive folds and are never difficult to put on. Look at the successful women around you and you'll notice that their clothing always looks as if it were made for them alone. Starting today, ignore size numbers when you shop. (If you are size 14 or under, the Chico's chain of stores kindly sizes its clothes from 0 to 3. Since when have size 14 gals been a size 3?) Most important, pay for alterations if you need them. Sure, it's unfair that men get them free while we have to pay, but it's absolutely worth the expense to make you look *rica*.

> *You are a beautiful Latina goddess.*
>
> Yasmin Davidds-Garrido, *author,* Empowering Latinas

> Loving what you've got means not complaining to anyone about your weight or shape, particularly at work.

Think "Line"

La rica look is all about projecting effortless style. To look *rica* is to look like you haven't tried too hard but have achieved a stunning effect. An easy way to do that is to create an unbroken line from head to toe. (Bonus: It makes short girls look taller.) This is achieved by making one color and its variations in hue the dominant one in your outfit, makeup, and accessories. It does *not* mean that you must dress head to toe in black. You can wear different intensities of the same color family, for instance, with small accents of another color to achieve the rich look. Or, if you are wearing a little black dress or pants suit, add a splash of color with a colorful blouse, scarf, pashmina, or necklace, but not all four unless they are in the same color family. Letting more than one color fight for dominance or mixing too many colors will detract from the professional, rich look. Make sure your hose and shoes blend in with your colors, too. Women who wear shoes and hose that are too different in tone from their outfits tend to look like legs walking by themselves.

You also should make sure that the top and bottom of your outfit don't fight with each other. The richest look is achieved by having these elements match, as long as they are solid colors. If you are going with a pattern (and make it a subtle one), let it be only on the top and make sure everything else is solid. Mixtures of patterns may be fashionable, but that doesn't mean that they project anything but confusion to the people who see you. "Did that *mujer* get dressed in the dark?" may be the kindest thought they'll have.

Accessories: Follow the Rule of 10

A long time ago I read somewhere that dressing with elegance can be achieved by following the "rule of 10." I've followed that rule ever since, and I believe it has enhanced my image immensely. Here's how it works: Once you get dressed, count every accessory you have on, including purse, briefcase, and watch. And yes, you must count each earring, finger ring, and piercing separately. Add an extra point for each print pattern you are wearing. Also add extra points for each thing that dangles or clanks. (In fact, you shouldn't wear anything distracting like that in a business setting.) Now count it up. If the result is more than 10, take something off until you get it down to that number. Remove a pattern. Take off a bracelet. Put some of your purse contents inside your briefcase and leave the purse at home. Or leave the briefcase: You don't want to do work at home every night, do you? Take off the extra extravagance in every area of your accessories. You'll be surprised at the difference "less is more" makes in your look. *La rica* look dazzles with a few carefully placed pieces; it does not go overboard with baubles, bangles, and beads.

> *I try to concentrate on getting good rest, because I do love what I do.*
>
> Jennifer Lopez, *actress*

Don't Be Casual about Casual Viernes.

Those who wish to look *rica* costume for casual Fridays very carefully. The good news for the image-conscious is that many employers are going back to weeklong professional dress codes, but even if your workplace still takes a casual attitude, you can use that to your advantage. To avoid looking too sloppy—or too sexy—try to achieve your Friday look by wearing matching Capri pants and blouse with strappy sandals instead of jeans or pleated khakis. Jeans are usually too tight for work, and pleated khakis tend to get wrinkled and baggy. (In fact, pleats should be abolished by law. They make *todo el mundo* look fat!) In the winter a well-fitting wool sweater set and pants with a kicky necklace looks casual without being stuffy. I am a firm believer that even casual clothes should match and look put together. Who knows when you'll be seen in action by someone influential?

Tone Down Hair, Nails, Perfume, and Makeup

When we Latinas make a mistake in the area of grooming, it's usually because we're too enthusiastic. Maria Christina, an *argentina* who has started a line of cosmetics especially for Latinas called Para Me, which will soon be available nationally, notices that tendency in many of her clients: "Our biggest mistake is applying makeup with a heavy hand. A little bit, applied well, is all we need because, in most cases, our features are more defined than those of *Anglas*. We need to highlight one feature at a time with makeup, not everything at once." Maria advises that Latinas choose their favorite feature and emphasize that. "But don't overemphasize your lips in most offices," she advises for obvious reasons, "unless you are selling lipstick." Or looking for a *novio*?

Women who look *rica* also take care of their nails and hair religiously. That means a manicure every two weeks, a pedicure regularly if you *ever* wear sandals, and a trip to the hair salon at least every three weeks. Nails need to be shortish (no claws) and conservatively colored to coordinate with your outfits for work, and hair needs to be trimmed as often as possible. The rich look means never having frizzies, partially grown-out color or processes, or a hairdo that doesn't . . . do. Successful women never seem to have a hair out of place, and this is how they do it. There is no shame in going to one of the cheaper haircutting places if you can't afford the salons the *rica* use. Use the money you save to have a really good color job done at a top-line salon every two months. (Ask someone whose color you really admire to refer you to her colorist.) A really great color—not too brassy or too blond—will give you a polish that can only enhance your image.

Ask for Help If You Need It

Women who "dress rich" all have one thing in common: Not a single thing is out of place or over the top. Yet they don't have to be boring or unfashionable. Instead, they pick and choose among current trends for looks that prove they are both professional and stylish. Admittedly, that's not the easiest thing to do. I often recommend to my employees that they use the services of the personal shoppers who are available at many department stores. These services are typically free and do not obligate you to buy anything. As long as you remember that the personal shopper's goal is to get you to spend money and have primed yourself to resist temptation, they can help you find clothes that enhance your image as an up-and-comer. Be sure to tell your shopper the image styles you need to match in your workplace and you'll be set to look *rica*.

Does *la rica* look mean that you must always wear a suit or can never follow fashion trends? Of course not. Extreme "power dressing," always wearing an unadorned boxy suit, is likely to backfire, in fact. By personal preference I wear a jacket almost every day in a work setting. But I save my expensive (not boxy) St. John suits for my most serious meetings, meetings where the guys are likely to be wearing their power suits too. I usually recommend to ambitious women that they buy one or two of the most expensive suits they can afford for such occasions and make sure the suits are tailored impeccably to fit. Even then I soften my look with a silk blouse, a bright scarf, or a silly pin.

I also spend time keeping up with fashion, mainly through magazines. By doing that, I can figure out how to update my look with a blouse or accessory so that I look up to the minute without looking like a slave to fashion. People who keep up with fashion admire me for staying current without spending a carload of cash, whereas those who could care less about fashion just perceive me as being creative and fresh.

THE DON'T LIST

One magazine's most popular page is the "Dos and Don'ts," a catalog of the frumpy, the fabulous, and the fashion victims caught on film by its roving cameraperson. We are fascinated by these pages because they show women in all their "glory" as they really look to the world. We're also secretly pleased because there is no way we could look as bad as these women do. Right? Uh huh. Think about what you're wearing right now. Would it look *maravilloso* in full color in a magazine? How about what you wore during your commute to work today? Would you have wanted to run into the CEO? I thought not.

There are certain things all of us are tempted to do sometimes for comfort, convenience, or whatever that you must lose the habit of doing if you are going to project a consistently rich image. Women who have *la rica* look practice it consistently and would never be caught dead committing these image killers.

- **Don't wear baggy clothes or clothes that are too tight.** Elegance means clothes that fit no matter what size you are. Baggy clothes draw attention to your size and whisper about your low self-image. Tight clothes send entirely the wrong message at work. Even if you are proud of your body, work is not the place to show it off. Clothes that neither cling nor bag are what you should be aiming for. Make friends with a good seamstress in your neighborhood and take your clothes to her for a nip here and a tuck there or find a department store that offers relatively inexpensive alterations for new purchases. It's a fact of life, *mujeres*, that almost none of the clothes we buy will fit right off the rack.

- **Don't be caught without spares.** A friend of mine always carries spare earrings in her car because she's always leaving the house with empty holes in her ears. (She hates mornings.) If you wear skirts, a spare pair of nylons needs to be tucked into your purse (not your desk, which could be miles away from where you need them). I also carry a spare scarf with me to important functions in case I accidentally dribble on the one I'm wearing. It can happen to anyone!

- **Don't carry a saddlebag.** You know what I mean. You probably are lugging a purse around every day that is much too big for your body. It detracts from your professionalism to drag that thing around, and the worst part is that you don't need half the stuff that's in there. Admit it: If you were permitted to carry only half of what you carry now, you'd figure out what to leave behind. Checkbook and credit cards? Why do you need both? All your credit cards? How many can you use at one time? Five lipsticks? How many lips do you have? You get the idea. In fact, why don't you try to get some of that weight out of your life? Starting today, eliminate half your burden and reward yourself with a cute little purse to carry what's left.

- **Don't forget the feet.** It seems that *mujeres* can't help going to extremes when it comes to shoes. They either schlep around in ugly, grubby gym shoes or cram their feet into ill-fitting but fashionable torture devices. Let's put it this way: Nobody should be seen in either kind of shoe. There are plenty of comfortable shoes, like those made by Rockport and Coach, that won't detract from your image even if you are just walking to work. And please save the stilletto, pointy-toe shoes for the evening if you must wear them. Wear them at work and people will wonder why you've spent so much on shoes that are obviously dysfunctional, and that may make them wonder about your decision-making capacity in other areas. Plus, you'll have to spring for bunion surgery twenty years from now and wear flat ugly shoes ever after, even in the evening. Trust me on this.

- **Don't trust every mirror.** If you don't have one, invest in a full-length mirror. A mirror showing your image only from the waist up is not enough to judge the impact of an entire outfit, shoes included. Also, be sure to check your face in a mirror that is lighted in the same way that your next setting will be. You need to adjust your look for fluorescent or stage lights, for instance, if an important appearance will take place beneath them. You'll look overdone in natural light afterward until you have time to adjust your makeup again, but you want your look to shine in the available lighting you have.

- **Don't ever let your inner barbarian escape.** People are watching your behavior all the time, especially at work. And that's too bad because few women or men learn at home anymore about how to behave in public. That means not putting on makeup at the table after eating even if every other woman is whipping out her lipstick. It means never chewing gum or smoking in public, especially at the front door of your building. (If you must smoke, take a walk.) It means not taking cell phone calls if you are with other people. It means not slurping or gobbling, surprisingly common behavior among even fairly polite young women. And it means knowing what fork and glass to use even if you have to watch what other people are doing before you pick yours up. In fact, you can learn a lot about how to act *rica* by observing people who are successful. Watch your image mentor closely. I'll bet my fortune that *she* is not a barbarian.

If you train yourself to look professional—and *rica*—you will always be prepared for any opportunity to get ahead. To take just a tiny example, it's been a long time since I've appeared anywhere outside my own bedroom without makeup. I won't even take my dog out for a walk around the block without at least putting on lipstick and a nice blouse. You never know who you might meet coming in the other direction.

> *Everything in nature is beautiful, so accepting who you are gives you the confidence you need to succeed in the business world.*
>
> Maria Cristina, *Para Me Cosmetics*

8
Making the Most of Your *Dinero*

When will you know you are *rica*? When you've made your first six-figure income? Your first million? Your first billion? Let me tell you: Some people never think they are *rica* enough. Other people are happy—and feel rich—on an average person's salary. It all depends on your attitude toward money, which is something you can improve on no matter how much (or how little) money you have. However, having a healthy attitude toward money is especially important if you plan to make a lot of money. In fact, it can make all the difference in determining whether you make the most of your money. Many of us think that winning the lottery or earning a six-figure income will solve all our financial problems. Yet having money can be the start of a different set of problems. I knew a family in California that won millions in the lottery not too long ago. The husband started a string of companies, trying to become even wealthier, but knew very little about running a business. Several years later they had spent all the lottery money and had to declare bankruptcy.

> *Having money can be the start of a different set of problems.*

I am not saying that all of us would run out and blow millions if we got our hands on that much money. Too few people, though, have the knowledge needed to be able to deal with the kind of financial success I hope this book will give you. Schools don't teach money management, and many parents are bad financial managers. In the United States today we save only 3 percent of our incomes on average. Even China is ahead of us in that area. In fact, I would bet my tax bill (which sometimes has six zeros on it) that most of you are carrying huge credit-card balances no matter what your income is. I know where you're coming from: I did the same thing. Money was something I couldn't be bothered to think about, and so I bought whatever I wanted and charged it. After all, I worked hard every day, didn't I? And I deserved a little reward for that, didn't I? *Claro*, I thought I did. My credit-card balances piled up, and I was always astounded that none of my raises made me feel more financially secure.

Does any of this sound like you? If it does—and I'm pretty sure it will since about half of us carry large credit-card balances—you'll want to pay attention to my advice about money. Why pay attention to me? Well, I had my financial house in order long before I became wealthy. In fact, I might not have become wealthy if I hadn't gotten a handle on it. If I hadn't started managing my *dinero*, I wouldn't have had any to invest when the Entravision deal came along. Those guys weren't going to take a credit card! Even now that I can afford to buy a Learjet, I always think about those poor Lotto winners and wonder whether my money will last. And then I take steps to make sure that it does. You can and should start taking those steps too. You'll be grateful you did.

Get your financial house in order.

YOU DON'T HAVE TO LIKE NUMBERS— JUST COLORS, LIKE GREEN

Think about it this way: If you don't manage your money, your money will manage you. You must take control of your money just as you would take a leadership role. You want to have systems and partnerships in place so that everything functions smoothly, without surprises. You want to have the means to take the calculated risks that are likely to bring you "luck." And you want to be able to take care of all the real needs—and many of the dreams—you and your family have. To do that you need to start with some *reglas fundamentales* and follow them every day. They're what I call my money mantras, and just like mantras in yoga, they can lead to deep inner wealth. (Deep in your bank account, that is!) I mean them very seriously. These thoughts are what helped me feel *rica* even when I was pretty *pobre*. Repeat them to yourself whenever your money (or lack of it) is making you crazy.

You need to start with some reglas fundamentales *and follow them every day.*

Money Mantra 1: Credit Cards Are Evil

Yes, evil. What else can you call something that says in effect, "Don't you want this pretty apple? Here, take a bite. Pay no attention to the fine print that says you'll have to give me a whole barrel of apples in return." Credit-card ads on television promise that the world will be at your feet if you'll only accept this wonderful piece of plastic. You only have to cover a low, low minimum payment each month to buy all the goodies you want, credit card companies say. And yet, like the snake in the

Garden of Eden, their promises are deceiving. For one thing, they charge obscenely high rates on the money they lend you so casually. Only credit-card companies and loan sharks have not reduced their finance charges significantly as interest rates have plummeted in the economy as a whole. Even "low-rate" cards charge 5 to 10 percent more than it costs the credit-card companies to obtain the money. Cards for people with less than perfect credit (or people who haven't shopped for a "good" rate) can be more than 20 percent higher than market interest rates. In fact, the average consumer pays 16 percent interest on credit-card balances. And that adds up to hundreds or thousands of dollars more per year that consumers must pay for the convenience of buying things they can't afford.

To make things worse, the *average* American consumer owed a whopping $8,940 in credit-card balances in 2002, according to CNN. If you make only the minimum payment of 2 percent each month on that balance, at 16 percent interest it will take you approximately 30 *years* to pay that kind of balance off. And that's if you don't buy anything new until then. To put it in a less depressing way, if you buy something that costs $1,000, charge it on a credit card, and pay only the minimum balance, you'll have paid for it in about fifteen years and it will have cost you about $2,500 to buy it. Still depressing, huh? Sorry, but it's meant to be.

I know what I'm talking about here. When I was starting out, when I was working three jobs and had just divorced, I thought credit cards were the answer to my prayers. I had every credit card ever invented, I think. Even K-Mart. I was one of those people who bought anything they wanted and paid only the minimum payment: $10 or $20 a month on each card. I thought I was doing great: snazzy clothes, nice things for my house, toys for the kids. My biggest downfall was Christmas, when I could prove how "successful" I was. But every year I was always still paying for the last Christmas when the next one came along. (Sound familiar?)

One day, though, when I was paying bills, trying to deal with another maxed-out card, I was horrified to realize: "I am never going to pay these things off!" That night I took a scissors to those cards. I kept only two: American Express because you *must* pay that one off every month and Visa because it really is accepted everywhere. I took out a second mortgage on my home (which is tax-deductible) and paid off my cards. And from that day forward I have always paid off the entire balance on those cards each month, no matter what. Knowing that I have to do that, even today, makes me think about whether I can afford each purchase every time I whip out my card. It's just that now I can afford to write a bigger check each month. Which leads to my first tip for feeling financially secure.

Consejo de Rico: *Pay Off Your Credit Cards Right Now*
If you are *not* paying credit-card finance charges, it's the same thing as earning 16 percent interest on an investment. Where in the heck can you earn that kind of money now that the stock market is in the tank? Nowhere. Paying off your credit cards is like having a license to print money. No matter what you have to put off buying for a few years, do it: It's that important. If you have a savings account, use it to pay off your cards. It makes no sense to earn 2 percent interest on your savings account if it's costing you 18 percent to carry a balance on your credit-card bill.

Consejo de Rico: *Have a Credit-Card-Shredding Fiesta*
Invite your friends to celebrate your newfound freedom from credit-card evil. Use a big kitchen shears to cut the cards into tiny bits. Throw the pieces around like confetti. *Cha-cha* on them. You may even be able to persuade some of your *amigas*

to follow your lead. (Tell them how much that new suit is really costing them to pay off on the credit-card plan.)

Money Mantra 2: The Little Stuff Adds Up

What difference can it make that you have a Starbucks mocha latte vente every morning rather than a cup of plain old boring coffee? Only about $5 per day. And lunch or dinner (or both) at a restaurant or by carryout will never break the bank, will it? Many of us, especially if we're being promoted regularly, soon start to look at $5, $10, or $20 purchases as hardly worth thinking about. And then we wonder, Where did that last raise go? Why am I not feeling wealthier than I did before I got that extra pay in my check? You are not wealthier because you've decided subconsciously that you "deserve to enjoy the pay you've earned" or "don't have time to cook anymore with all my responsibilities." Both ideas are valid, and I believed them for years. But here's an eye-opener: Put a little notebook in your purse and use it to write down every purchase you make this week. Start tomorrow. At the end of each day add up what you've spent. If you're like me, you will be floored by the amount of *dinero* that has slipped through your fingers almost unnoticed. You'll also find, if you look closely, that quite a few of your purchases were not really things you needed but only "I gotta have that"s. We all know that many of these purchases, especially if they are made when we're shopping with our girlfriends, just end up cluttering our closets. They're the kinds of things we buy to look good in front of other people.

It's the desire to "look *linda* to others" and "live the easy life" that ensures that so few people become *rica* even if they make good money. In the enlightening book *The Millionaire Next Door,* marketing professors Thomas Stanley and William Danko examined the habits of weathy people. They found that most wealthy people do *not* make a show of their money or indulge themselves with expensive purchases. In fact, they discovered that "many people who live in expensive homes and drive luxury cars do not actually have much wealth.... Wealth is not the same as income. If you make a good income each year and spend it all, you are not getting wealthier. You are just living high." A millionaire, they found, is more likely to be living in the most average house in *your* neighborhood.

Most wealthy people do not make a show of their money or indulge themselves with expensive purchases.

I agree with those authors even though I have purchased a couple of nice homes since I made my bucks. But I still believe in buying only what I *need*. I will never own a Learjet. I never even fly first-class unless I can get a *free* frequent-flyer upgrade. I still don't go out for dinner very often at fancy restaurants. Instead, I do what I did when I was still coming up in my career: I often make a week's worth of dinners ahead of time so that I never have the handy excuse of being "too tired to cook." And I always know or can easily find out how much I can spend in a month because I religiously do what I'm about to tell you to do.

Consejo de Rico: *Give Yourself an Allowance*
That's right. I live on an allowance every month, and I like it! It keeps me from worrying about my money and allows me to spend for fun things too, as long as I don't get carried away. When I was living from paycheck to paycheck, my allowance gave me some confidence that emergencies wouldn't flatten me. And now that confidence keeps me from worrying—even subconsciously—that I'm going to end up homeless and poor again. Yes, I really do worry about that. Many women do.

Oprah Winfrey told *Fortune* magazine a couple of years ago that she keeps $50 million in cash as her "personal bag lady fund."

How do you put yourself on an allowance that doesn't make you feel like a *niña* again? *Primero, pay yourself first.* Even $50 or $100 a week going into savings (or to pay off credit cards) can add up. And that emergency fund is going to grow faster the more you can put into it. To figure out how much you can afford to save (and spend), look at your expenses with a microscope. Figure out *inmediatamente* the fixed amount you pay regularly every month, for things like rent/mortgage, loans, condo fees, and car payments. Then look back in your checkbook over the last year to see the average amount you spent on variable expenses such as utilities, phone, groceries, and other survival needs that do not cost the same every month.

These regularly occurring fixed and variable costs are the "nut" you have to cover, the expenses that come up every month. Once you know what your nut is, you can easily tell how much you are likely to have left for your allowance each month. Your allowance covers such things as business clothes, dinners out, parties, and other things that are "nice" to buy but not essential. Decide what a reasonable amount for these expenses is, one that will never bust your budget, and give that to yourself to spend every month.

If you find you are overspending your income and can't afford to give yourself an allowance, you can make some rational choices now about where to cut back. What can you most easily give up? The expensive cell phone plan that allows you to call each and every friend and talk forever about nothing? Your six dinners out every week? Your St. Johns and Manolo Blahniks? Start there and keep paring away until your nut plus your allowance plus your savings/credit-card payoff equals your income.

Fortunately, this allowance idea is not really about giving things up. Even when I was poor, I always made sure my allowance had one item in it that made me feel *rica*: I call it *guilt-free money* (GFM). I can spend my GFM any way I choose without thinking about it for an instant. Thus, even on an allowance, I don't have to give up Starbucks. But when my GFM for the month is gone, I force myself to wait until the next month to get another latte even though I have enough money to offer to buy a piece of the company. *Ay*, does that coffee taste good when you have to wait for it!

Consejo de Rico: *Pay Your Bills When They Arrive*
This is another tip that can make you feel really *rica*. Rich people don't have to worry about paying their bills. You can stop worrying about bills when you put yourself on an allowance. You know how much you're going to pay out each month and how much guilt-free money you have to spend, and so you can pay every bill as it comes in the door without worrying about whether you'll have "too much month left at the end of your money." If a bill is much bigger than you expect, take the difference out of your allowance or savings. Just be sure to pay yourself back as soon as possible.

> *I learned that money can be ephemeral—here today and gone tomorrow—so we must learn how to enjoy [it]. Remember, the important things in life are still free.*
>
> Cristina Saralegui,
> *Univision talk show host*

Money Mantra 3: Don't Automatically Spend a Raise

Isn't it funny how every time we earn more money, we find more stuff to spend it on? Somehow the bigger salary slips through our fingers just as easily as the old one did. How does that happen? Oh, yes, of course: We've got to buy better-quality clothes to look the part. And we have to get our hair done at a better salon or highlighted in two shades of blond. Or something. But deep down we sometimes hear that little voice whispering, "You're making this kind of money and still have to worry about how you're going to afford to repair the car if it breaks down? And what happens if you get a big doctor bill that the insurance won't cover? What will you do then, Miss Just-Got-a-Raise?" *Sí*, that little voice that sounds so much like *su mamá*.

The way to quiet the voice of worry is to start building up a nest egg for emergencies and for your future. Every month you should pay yourself first by putting money into savings or paying off credit cards, as I mentioned in the mantra above. But in addition you should *pledge to save 5 or 10 percent of any raise you get*. The easy way to do that is to have it removed from your check through payroll deduction. If you never see it, you'll never be able to spend it. Check with the human resources department about how to get this done. And while you're there find out about your company's "pretax" retirement plans. Stock market upheavals and corporate shenanigans have given 401(k) and other benefit plans a bad name. And you are right to be cautious, especially if your company's plan forces you to invest in company stock. However, if you are cautious, these plans can add significantly to your wealth because of two factors: First, the money you invest builds up tax-free; second, if your company matches your contribution, you can as much as double your money instantly and completely without risk!

Consejo de Rico: *Figure Out What's Important*

Starting to save "someday" has a way of not happening. There's always something the kids need, a great new *cosa* to buy, a dream vacation to take. But what about the kids' college education, the bigger home you want, and your retirement? The same way I advised you to set goals for your career, you should set goals for your financial future. It may seem that the future is far, well, in the future. Trust me: It is closer than you think. People who become "millionaires next door" decide early on what is important to them. Do they need a McMansion in a hot part of town? If so, that's what they work hard for and save their raises for. If it's more important to give their kids a great start in life and then retire to an exciting corner of the world, that's what they set their sights on. Remember, when you give yourself an allowance, you don't have to shortchange the kids now or deprive yourself. You only have to set priorities about what's important to you and your family. Then your finances will almost take care of themselves.

Money Mantra 4: Never Pay Retail

In my opinion, you can never be too rich to pass up a sale. It feels so good to save money and still get what you want. I feel that there is *absolutamente* no reason to pay full price for something that will be marked down if you wait a little while. Who wants to buy winter coats in August anyway, when they first appear in the stores? However, you don't want to be stuck with racks of ugly, picked-over merchandise to choose from either. I've found that the best strategy is to make friends with the salesclerks at my favorite stores. Have them notify you when the new season's lines come in so that you can choose things you want. Then have them keep an eye on your favorites and call you when they go on sale. They'll do you that favor if you often reward them by coming in and buying the things you were interested in.

I also look for bargains wherever I can find them. If you're ever in Denver, don't get in my way when TJ Maxx has its sales.

I'm always amazed at the prices you can get there on really good-looking clothes. I also buy in bulk, to this day. Many Latinas associate buying in bulk with the habits of country cousins who went back to the old country to buy carloads of cheap stuff to bring home. The Latina author Sandra Cisneros writes about her humiliation at being dragged along on such trips in her recent novel *Caramello*. But it's not just *campesinos* who stock up on staples at the warehouse store. I do it all the time and never considered dropping the habit when I became wealthy. It saves a lot of time to buy a 50-pound bag of flour and a 10-gallon jar of olives all at once rather than going back to the store ten times, and you always know you'll have something to eat when your hungry *primos* drop by!

> *It's not just* campesinos *who stock up on staples at the warehouse store.*

Consejo de Rico: *Don't Waste Time to Save Money*

I will never drive two hours to get to a sale. I will never shop at a flea market except to have fun. And I especially won't clip coupons. Think about the time you can spend clipping, filing, and finding coupons at the store and then think about what you earn per hour. Are you saving more than it's costing you in time? That's something economists call opportunity cost, and if you're wasting time that you could spend earning money (or resting to make more money tomorrow), whatever you are doing to save money is not worth the trouble.

Money Mantra 5: Buy "a Little Casa"

I was 22 years old, with two little babies, when my husband and I bought our first house. It was just a *pequeña* ranch house, pretty ugly actually, but we weren't choosy because we knew it was just a starter house. We had saved some money for a down payment and borrowed some from my husband's parents. My *mami* almost had a fit, though, because she thought we were getting into debt way over our heads. (Actually, the payment was $67 a month, which shows you how long ago *that* was.) But we had planned carefully how to afford it and how to pay back my in-laws' loan as soon as possible, and we did.

I believed then and believe now that home ownership is one of the smartest things anyone can do to build wealth. A landlord can't evict you or raise the rent, although you can be thrown out on the street if you don't pay your mortgage. And your money just goes out the window when you pay rent. With a mortgage, though, part of every payment goes to pay down your mortgage balance, building the percentage of the home that you actually own (your equity).

Home ownership is one of the smartest things anyone can do to build wealth.

Consejo de Rico: *Buy Less House Than You Can Afford*
If you can afford it, a 15-year mortgage builds your equity faster, meaning that you'll profit more when you sell. But payments are higher on a 15-year mortgage than on a conventional 30-year mortgage. Consider a 15-year mortgage along with your other options as you think about what to buy: Perhaps you'll want to buy a smaller house than you can afford so that you can pay if off faster with a 15-year mortgage.

At the same time, don't listen to a mortgage banker who says that you can afford to pay 40 percent of your income for housing (mortgage, taxes, and insurance). Forty percent! Unfortunately, many bankers encourage clients to take on this much debt. Don't listen. Take on only the level of debt you are comfortable with even if it means settling for a tiny house. You should be looking for a house you can afford *right now*, no matter how much money you plan to make in the future. Remember, your real estate agent earns a bigger commission for selling you a bigger house, and so many agents try to sell you the biggest house they can. Find a real estate agent who understands how much you want to pay each month and won't push you to look at houses that will cost more than that.

Money Mantra 6: Take Sensible Risks

As with your career, you are going to get farther with your money if you take sensible risks. *Claro*, you're never going to get rich by putting all your money in a savings account. These days savings accounts earn 3 percent if you're lucky. But with the stock market meltdown of the last few years, many Latinas would rather put their money in a mattress than invest in the stock market. Well, guess what? This is exactly the right time to invest, after so many stocks have been beaten down from their completely unrealistic heights of the 1990s.

Should you run out and invest in the next hot stock you hear a coworker raving about? Most assuredly not. By the time Stanley in the next cube has heard about that "great deal," so has the rest of the world. (Besides, he probably heard about it on CNBC, where some of the stock gurus are well known to be personally involved as brokers of the stocks they tout.) In fact, you should be suspicious of any deal that promises higher returns than most people are getting. I shake my head when I hear news stories about people being duped into giving money to people offering fantastic returns. "Well, it was good old Bob from church. We never dreamed he would lie to us!" It's amazing how many good old Bobs there are out in the world (and *amistoso Rodrigos* too), and they always seem to find willing victims, no matter how often rip-off stories hit the news.

Instead of relying on dubious advice, it's important for you, as a leader, to begin taking sensible risks on your own. Here are some ways to begin getting the most for your money risk.

1. **Don't invest in *either* individual stocks or a savings account.** The first is too risky because you could lose your shirt, and the second is not risky enough to earn you anything. Instead, stash your savings in a low-cost mutual fund, such as those from Vanguard or Fidelity. (Never invest in a mutual fund, though, without investigating its record fully. The mutual fund industry has been rocked by revelations of unethical conduct among many of the largest companies.) You want a mutual fund that promises steady returns with minimum risk. Look for an index fund, an equity-income fund, or an income fund. You can build up a nice nest egg if you "pay yourself first" and stick as much as you can afford to into your chosen mutual fund. You'll learn to love receiving the monthy statements as you watch your investment grow. And grow it will. Average stock market returns over time are still way above those for interest-bearing accounts. Investors really are rewarded for taking reasonable risks with their money.

2. **If you don't have health insurance, get some *ahora mismo*.** Your cheapest option is a major medical policy with a high deductible (the amount you must cover before your coverage kicks in). It won't cover doctor or emergency room visits, but you don't risk going into unmanageable debt if a family member becomes seriously ill or is injured badly. You can find a good list of plans to start with at www.insurance.com

3. **Diversify.** People who lose their shirts through investments usually have put too many *huevos* in one basket. As you begin finding more money to invest, look for creative ways to put it to work. Put some in real estate, some in stocks, and some in safe, interest-bearing accounts. Then invest in businesses or start your own business. Back a promising musician or artist. Yes, those last suggestions can be quite risky, but if you don't tie up too much of your nest egg in any single investment, you can lose only a small fraction of your worth if something goes wrong with one of them. Diversity means less risk overall while still making a big win possible.

MONEY FOR TWO: WHY IS MANAGING FAMILY MONEY SO HARD?

I'll admit it: I've never thought that handling money is sexy. Or fun. Or even very interesting. In fact, almost everyone probably would rather think about something else. Buying stuff, *sí*. Money management, *no*. Ho, hum. However, I have trained myself to take an interest in money because it is so important to my success, and I am certain other Latinas can follow my example to get their financial houses in order. Unfortunately, many Latinas also struggle against a *cultura* that can make money management doubly difficult, indeed, a source of family conflict. We hear this *cultura* all around us as we begin to be successful and even from the little voice inside our heads. The voices whisper, "Who do you think you are to be such a big shot about money?" The voices imply that if you make plans for your money, you are acting above your station, getting too big for your *pantalones*. You, as a woman, shouldn't bother your pretty head about money, after all. You should leave it to those who are older, wiser, more manly than you.

Many Latinas also struggle against a cultura *that can make money management doubly difficult.*

¡Es muy incorrecto! First of all, you must recognize that no matter how much you love your guy today, you might get divorced. Fifty percent of marriages end that way nowadays. If you leave all the money decisions to the "man of the house," you may be setting yourself up for a hard fall, *cara*. Your husband (or your ex) could "forget" to pay his life insurance premium as mine did right before he died, so that his daughters got nothing. He could be withdrawing money from your joint accounts, perfectly legally. He could be running up huge credit-card bills, which you could end up being responsible for if your name is on the account. Same thing with income taxes. If you sign a joint tax return that contains lies, you could be on the hook to the government for back taxes, interest, and penalties even if you divorce him later and even if you didn't know anything about the lies! The point is not to say that your *novio* is doing these things. It is that he *could* be and you'll never know it unless you take responsibility for understanding your family's finances. Whether you like numbers or not, you owe it to yourself to become informed or you may owe money to the government!

Still, many Hispanics, including many supposedly "modern" husbands, expect that the man of the house will both make the money and spend the money. Like your *mamá*, you may be asked to make do with what's left. "I make the money, so it's up to you to make sure it covers everything" is still heard in too many Hispanic households. Meanwhile, *el marido* is out buying a hot little sports car with the money *he* earns. Shouldn't it be different in households where both spouses work? In some households it is, but a surprising number of Latinas still live with men who, perhaps unconsciously, expect to be the master of the bank account. You probably know some of these men or live with one yourself. Can you remember an instance when your *novio* seemed excessively put out when you argued about buying something he wanted that you didn't consider necessary? Did you wonder where all the hurt feelings came from? It's *la cultura*, especially television, which tells him he is not an *hombre* unless he can spend his (your family's) money as he pleases.

> Many Latinas still live with men who, perhaps unconsciously, expect to be the master of the bank account.

Especially if you are earning more money than your *esposo* does, he may find it very difficult to share money decisions unless you can persuade him to love you enough to form a real partnership with you when it comes to money. Most couples simply don't talk about their attitudes toward *dinero*. You may be the kind of person who wants to know your bank balance to the penny and fears that any financial setback could leave you homeless. (As irrational as that fear may be as you climb the corporate ladder, you will never lose it.) Many women who grew up poor feel that way. Your *novio* could be the kind who forgets to write down checks and spends like there's no tomorrow. Or your roles could be reversed.

One thing is sure, though: Studies show that you are likely to marry someone who looks at money differently than you do. Spenders are attracted to savers and vice versa, financial harmony be damned, until after you leave the altar. Then watch out. Maybe we unconsciously seek someone to help us control our worst tendencies. (Savers aren't much fun left to their own devices, and yes, many spenders feel guilty about the misery they cause around them.) But if we don't take the time to talk about what's important to us financially, it's certain that we'll be spending it yelling instead.

Still, you may have trouble finding the mental energy for a conversation that could begin with "Honey, can you tell me everything about why you're so dumb about money?" A better approach, say certified financial planners such as Richard Tanner, a partner in the Koptis Organization in Cleveland, is to take the time to create a family money statement. Tanner uses this concept to help wealthy clients with estates of $1 million or more plan to use their money in the best way, but it's just as useful for Latinas at any point in their careers. Just like the mission statements you encounter at work, this one is intended to state agreed-on goals in order to give you something to shoot for. Unlike many company mission statements, it is meant to be a realistic reflection of your lives. After all, you are not crafting it to impress investors or clients, only to guide you toward blissful financial couplehood. Sigh.

To create a family money statement, take some time to discuss the following questions thoroughly. Take all the time you need, perhaps over several long "working" dinners that you plan in advance. Relax. Open a bottle of wine. You may want to use a tape recorder if you don't want to take detailed notes. Don't criticize each other's answers; neither of you can help what your attitudes are. You come to marriage with money ideas that are deeply ingrained because of your experience with your parents. You are trying to learn how to work together to decide on and reach your financial goals. Think compromise and remember that you love the penny-pincher or spendthrift you are talking to. Here's another mantra to repeat if the going gets rough: "He may be crazy, but I love him!" If you are only thinking about getting married, it should be obvious by now that this can be a great exercise that could save you a lot of grief later on.

What's Your Money Mission? (Questions for Couples)

1. Were your parents good at managing money? Bad? In what ways?

2. Do you manage money differently than they did? Why?

3. What is the one change you would make to our family's finances right now?

4. How much income would you need to feel financially free?

5. How important is it to pay bills on time? To avoid interest charges and late fees?

6. What makes you feel rich? Buying whatever you want? Having money in the bank?

7. Are charities or good causes important to you? Would you like to make donations to them?

8. Do you prefer to save for big purchases or put them on a credit card today?

9. If you had a lot of money, what would you do with it and why?

You'll undoubtedly think of other questions to discuss. Think back to the big blowouts you and your *novio* have had about money. Be honest with yourself about what was behind your defensiveness and then explore his. Your goal should be to get to the bottom of your feelings about money and your goals for the future. Eventually you'll want to produce a written statement something like this, the more specific the better:

Ramirez Family Money Statement

We agree that it is important for our family to be debt-free, with the exception of our mortgage. But if we do borrow, we will never take on payments that are more than 25 percent of our take-home pay. Our goal is to open a home-cooking restaurant in ten years or less and use the value of our home to finance the start-up costs. We'll save 10 percent of our pay every month, pay down our mortgage as quickly as possible, and set aside $300 per month for each of us to play with, no questions asked. Starting in ten years, we'll save enough to send the kids to state colleges. And we'll retire to a sunny place when we've got at least $750,000 in investments or profit from the business. ¡Vamos!

You'll be surprised how many fewer arguments you have once you can pull out your mission statement and "remind" your partner what you agreed on. Every once in a while sit down (in a Jacuzzi?) and discuss your mission again. Needs change, goals change, and your mission can change along with them, without strife, as long as you do it as a couple.

Money Management for Singles

Everything I just said goes for singles too. You simply don't have the extra burden of having to work to get another person's agreement. However, you also do not have the support a spouse can provide in helping you reach your goals. Are you going to work three jobs the way I did when I got divorced, or are you going to decide which expenditures are really important to you? Knowing what your financial goals are is especially important to singles, who have only themselves to depend on when it comes to making ends meet. Sit yourself down with a glass of merlot and write your own money mission statement. Won't it be handy to have when a guy claiming to be Mr. Right comes along? "You're saving to buy a Harley? Yee-haa, so am I!"

Getting the Help You Need

Odds are that you didn't grow up wealthy. If you had, you wouldn't need a book to learn how to make it big. You'd simply wake up one morning to discover that you were the star of a blockbuster movie—or president—and think it was your talent alone that got you there. People who grow up wealthy also don't need to think about getting help to manage their money. From birth, they are surrounded by armies of accountants, attorneys, and advisers who tell them the right moves to make. This level of help is one of the primary reasons why there's great truth in the statement "the rich just get richer."

What kind of financial training did the rest of us have? We saw *mami* keeping the rent money in a coffee can (or in a no-interest checking account). We saw *papi* investing in "no-lose" business deals that always seemed to lose. Or if our parents were good money managers, they may have made us afraid to take any risks with our money because they always worried so much about money. Very few of us learned at home or in school what to do with money once it started flowing in faster than we could spend it.

Almost immediately after I started working in television, I started to get the feeling that my money was outrunning my ability to keep it on a leash, and so I decided to ask a team of "trainers" to help me, just as I would do if my dog were misbehaving. The first person I hired was my wonderful stockbroker, Steve Velasquez of Morgan Stanley Dean Witter (and his talented associate, Michael Chinn). Even though I had very little to invest at first, my stockbroker took an interest in helping me find the most appropriate investments for my small amount of money. To find a stockbroker or financial planner of your own like that, especially when so many of them are in the news these days for ripping off their clients, talk to people in your network who invest. (If you don't know who they are, make this a topic for small talk for the next few months.) Get the names of a few money managers and interview them. Are they intensely focused on you and your needs, or do they seem put off by the smallness of your nest egg? Invest a small amount with the one or two who make you feel most comfortable and intelligent. Yes, you want to feel intelligent around them, and you will if they aren't putting you down.

You also should also find an accountant, an insurance agent, and an attorney on the same basis. Why do you need all these potentially expensive people now? Simple. They'll save you a lot of money over the years if you take advantage of their expertise. The accountant may charge you a couple of hundred dollars for doing your taxes but should save you at least that much by making sure you take advantage of all the legitimate tax savings to which you are entitled. Storefront services such as H&R Block will be inadequate for you once your money life becomes the least bit complex. Having an accountant is well worth it unless you plan to memorize the 46,000-page federal tax code!

An insurance agent is vital too, especially if you have kids. You never know what's going to happen to you, and so you need life and disability insurance that is adequate for your family's needs if you're no longer around to provide for them. How do you know what's "adequate"? That's what the insurance agent will figure out for you. You need homeowner's or renter's insurance for much the same reason. You never know when a financial disaster is going to strike. You may never need your insurance—lucky you—but buying it after you need it is not an option. A good agent can save you thousands of dollars, a really valuable service at a time when insurance premiums are going through the roof. You may even discover that you can afford much more coverage than you thought. As with the other helpers, it pays to shop around until you feel comfortable and able to afford the coverage.

Finally, you should decide on an attorney, especially if you have kids. You may not want to think about it, but it is *muy importante* to name a guardian for them if something should happen to you. Would you want your crazy sister-in-law raising your children? That could happen if you don't name a guardian and if the court decides she's a fit mother for them. You'd rather have your friend Angelica raise them, but you don't get to choose her if you don't state it legally. And whether or not you have children, you'll also want a say in where your *dinero* goes after you're gone. You can do that if you plan ahead with an attorney.

This becomes even more vital when you have more money or if you ever start a business. My attorney not only put into writing where my money goes, he's saving me taxes today. Using a device called a charitable remainder trust, which is allowed under laws too complicated for me to understand, he saves me money on my income taxes, lets me provide an inheritance for my family, and makes sure the rest goes to my favorite charities. I don't like to think about a time when I won't be here anymore, but not thinking about it doesn't make that prospect go away. Just get an attorney you trust and throw it in his or her lap. Then you really won't have to think about it anymore.

Then take one final step to make sure you are never taken advantage of: *Take your advisers to lunch*—together. Introduce them if they don't already know one another, have a fun lunch, and then talk turkey. Let them know that you'll be showing any proposal you get from any of them to at least one of the others. Good advisers will be glad you did this since they like to coordinate plans with others so that they can get the best possible results for you. You'll never hear from dishonest advisers again; they don't want anyone looking over their shoulders.

Whether you are just starting out or have started to make it big, managing your *dinero* properly is vital to your mental health. There is nothing worse than being awake all night with money worries. In fact, lying awake worrying about money is likely to sabotage your efforts to move ahead with your career. Who wants to hire/promote/invest in someone who is desperate about money?

It's been years since I really worried about money, and I stopped worrying long before I had enough money to make me financially free. It's all a matter of attitude. If you control your actions and thoughts about money, it can't control you. Then you'll have the time you need to both set the world on fire and make it a better place.

9
Money Isn't Everything

*A*chieving *la vida rica* is a wonderful thing, but the rich life isn't really about money. In the end, money cannot make anyone happy despite what the Lotto ads say. Sure, it's great to be able to afford four homes and 300 pairs of shoes. I love visiting my shoes in my walk-in closets and adding to my collection whenever I feel like it. I even treated myself to a $300,000 shopping spree in Italy once just because I could. Being able to do stuff like that is so far removed from my childhood as a migrant worker that sometimes I have to pinch myself to realize that this is really *my* life. As Mae West once said: "I've been rich and I've been poor, and rich is better." Yet if I didn't have the money, *I would* still be happy and would still have *la vida rica* because I learned along the way to strive for success while building my life around the things that are important: family, community, and inner peace.

> *If I didn't have the money, I* would *still be happy.*

You too have to think about how you can go *beyond* material and personal success wherever you are in the journey toward achieving it. Beyond success? *Sí.* You must look beyond getting to the top of your profession, making a lot of money, earning the respect of your colleagues, and being a beloved boss. You must even look beyond your *pasión* because if you don't, you run the risk of becoming too focused on the day-to-day grind of constant work.

Success-oriented people are very good at putting their heads down and getting the job done. They are less accomplished at *getting the life done.* The most driven among us become workaholics almost by default, unable to break free from our electronic leashes, nervous when we don't check e-mail or voice mail, guilt-ridden if we leave important work undone at the office. Is any of this beginning to sound *familiar*? We tend to get so caught up in moving up the corporate ladder, working as many hours as we think we must to shine and get noticed by higher-ups. Gradually, you put your life on hold and tell your kids *"lo siento, m'ijos,"* (sorry, kids) over and over because "mommy has to work today." Or you make everybody miserable because you're so tired when you get home that you don't have the energy to put your whole heart into family time. The most you can do is call Domino's for a pizza. I know where you're coming from. I did exactly the same thing on my way to the top until one day something tragic happened that opened my eyes: *Mi querido papá* died suddenly at the relatively young age of 62.

My dad never took a vacation in his life because he had eight of us to feed. But he was all right with that, he said, because he was going to buy a Winnebago when he retired and see the world. The poor guy was still working when he died and never got a chance to go anywhere. He wouldn't have wanted us to grieve about that because he enjoyed the life he had. What happened to him, though, made me face reality. We are here for such a short time that we can't afford to promise ourselves or others that we'll give ourselves a rich life "someday." It occurred to me shortly after his death that no matter how hard you work, the reward you get is going to be the same as long as you get the job done well enough. *Por eso*, striving for perfection and making yourself crazy over having every *tilde* in place are only going to make your life a crazed series of crises.

This is especially true if you have heavy family responsibilities, as I did at that time. As a single mother, I always felt guilty about leaving my girls to go to work *and* leaving work to be with the girls. The respected New York–based research organization Catalyst, which studies women, has found that this problem is common among Latinas. A full 21 percent of Latinas in a 2002 study told Catalyst that they felt family responsibilities, including elder care, were a barrier to their advancement. One recommendation the group made was for bosses to "focus on productivity rather than time in the office. Establish explicit performance expectations." *¡Precisamente!* That's exactly what needs to happen, except that you can't count on your boss to do it for you. You have to take that final step in being the boss of your own career and *give yourself* the life you want at work and beyond. That is, you must consciously create the life you want both at work and in your free time.

Three-quarters of Latinos are confident that their children will have better jobs and make more money than they do.

CREATING THE LIFE YOU WANT

I've given you a lot of advice about how to create the life you want at work. But if your downtime is chaotic or unsatisfying, the best advice in the world won't make you a success at work. To a great degree, though, many of the same strategies that help people prosper in the business world also work on the home front.

Set Family Goals and Take Risks

Families can have annual goals just as businesses do. Otherwise your family may have only a lot of "shoulda, coulda, wouldas" to look back on when it comes time for the kids to leave the nest. Yes, we shoulda taken that vacation to Puerto Rico to see where our family came from, but there was never enough time. *Sí*, we coulda all taken riding lessons together, but we could never coordinate our schedules in time to sign up for classes. *Sin pregunta*, it woulda been nice to learn *abuela*'s recipes before she passed on.

Of course, family goals don't just happen, especially when everyone in the family has competing needs and preferences. You don't want to go on a vacation where the kids spend the whole time playing video games and never look at the scenery. It's just as well that you as parents aren't forced into something that will leave you snarling with boredom either. It's vital to set aside some relaxation time, arranged in advance, to talk about what's important to everyone. Design your family goal setting like a brainstorming session at work where everyone's ideas are considered valid and no one is allowed to criticize or ridicule the ideas of others. Search for common ground that will allow every member of the family to enjoy together time but allow each family member to bring the rest of you along on one top-priority activity. You want to encourage all the family members to stretch themselves—to take a risk and try something new—as much as possible in the safe environment of the family.

The same technique works for planning weekend activities as well. Sit down regularly with your family (over pizza?) and decide what fun things you should do over the next few months. Keep a calendar handy to schedule all of your individual "obligations," then figure out how to get out of several of them so you can have at least one weekend day a month for family togetherness. (Visits to relatives don't count.) Even if you just visit the Y together, make sure its something everyone can enjoy and your family will work hard to ensure that you get the stress break you need.

Let Everyone Work Up to His or Her Abilities

As you become more successful at work, the temptation is to "let somebody else do it" at home. So you hire a maid service and a gardener and a painter and then wonder why the kids are so surly. I was brought up on hard work and believe that it is good for kids (and *novios*) to be expected to work. If everything is done for you, you grow up expecting to be waited on. That is not a healthy attitude, especially in boy children who want to stay married. Thus, despite your temptation to do less work for yourself at home, I advise against hiring too much help. Instead, give each member of the family a chance to choose from a list of several jobs to do every day before you start assigning jobs. (Just one week doing the jobs *you* assign should arouse their interest in managing the workload themselves.) This self-management of chores may be their first experience of participatory management, where they are in charge of setting the duties and responsibilities. Don't be excessively concerned about the quality of the "output," at least at first, but do be creative in designing rewards for work that is especially well done and give them when they are least expected.

[My mother] told us growing up: "When you make it, when you are successful, you have an obligation to turn around and help those who are struggling, because this country has been so good to you."

Rep. Linda Sanchez *(D-Calif.)*

Share Everything

Secrets are as corrosive at home as they are in companies. It is my firm conviction that both parents and management can share 95 percent of the information they have in their possession. In both cases personal information about individual members of the "firm" should be kept under wraps and revealed only with permission. Beyond that, though, all but the youngest kids should know the facts about every situation that relates to the family and should be introduced to the family finances no matter what shape they are in. I believe that I learned an exceptional amount that helped me succeed in business by being involved in helping my parents manage their money. If there's something embarrassing about the way you manage money—or your family situations—what better excuse to do something about them than getting ready to share them with your kids? Every action you and your husband take with regard to your family then will be informed by the thought "What will the kids say about this when we tell them?" Not a bad watchdog to have.

Wear the Falda (Skirt) in the Family

If you have an *esposo*, you want him to help you up the ladder of success. It's that much harder to climb if you have a husband pulling you down with demands and misbehavior. That's a major reason I got rid of mine—a viable option for ambitious women but not one I would recommend if you can help it. What works best, in my observation, is a relationship built on the mutual ability to compromise and cooperate. Having demands all go one way or the other leads to resentment and hostility. Saying yes as often as possible, in contrast, builds respect and a well of goodwill to draw on in tough times as long as your spouse says yes equally as often. That is not to say that your *esposo* will behave this way unless you explain it to him. Too many of our husbands, especially the Latinos, were raised by mothers who couldn't do enough for their *hijos*. For those husbands, continual retraining, just as you would do with a thick-headed employee, is called for, along with a system of rewards. That's where "wearing the *falda*" comes in, if you get my drift. Feminine affection—and not just in bed—goes a long way toward establishing positive behavioral changes in the subject population.

> *Too many of our husbands, especially the Latinos, were raised by mothers who couldn't do enough for their hijos.*

Keep Your Friends Close and Your Family Closer

Your *amigas* are vital to your success: They'll tell you the truth when you need to hear it and prop you up when you're down. Your best friends will support you in everything you do, eagerly offering to help. Latinas are so good at treasuring their friends that I shouldn't even have to bring this up. However, when we climb the ladder of success, keeping our friends can become problematic. You have to go out of your way to keep in touch regularly and not withdraw because you are busy. If you can't carve out time to see everyone individually, at least keep in touch through personal e-mails and throw a big *fiesta* a couple of times a year. It can't hurt to help your friends meet each other even if they come from different walks of life. If they like you, it's almost certain that they'll like each other. Just don't feel the need to impress anyone as your status grows. Make it your goal to make everyone feel *cómodo* in your presence, comfortable and warm.

> *When we Latinas climb the ladder of success, keeping our friends can become problematic.*

But what can you do if your friends get jealous of you or feel that you've gotten too big for your britches? When they try to claw you back down? What can we do when members of our families do the same thing? Unfortunately, some will. It's an especially common attitude in the Hispanic community, where the reaction to the great luxury car you can afford now is likely to be *"¿Como se cree?"* (Who does she think she is?).

Los Angeles financial planner Louis Barajas has experienced that in his own life, coming from the *barrio* in East LA, and he hears it frequently from his Hispanic clients, male and female. "Latinas and Latinos have the culturally conditioned reaction that if you are successful, you are leaving your family and friends behind," he said recently. This is such a problem among his clients that Barajas has written a book called *The Latino Journey to Financial Greatness*. In it he talks about the "scarcity syndrome" that has infected many of our friends and family members. It's like we think we've been given a pie to eat and once it's gone, it's gone. If you get a big piece, if you get rich, that means I may get none. People who grew up poor or middle-class may be embarrassed to admit this, but every time they become jealous of someone else's success and try to kid that person into being ashamed of it, they are unconsciously saying: "You've made it big, but I know I can't." But there is no

> *I would certainly like to see our society reach a point where [being] the first of anything is no longer of relevance, because we are everyplace.*
>
> Ida Castro, *first Hispanic head of the EEOC, under President Clinton*

reason why your friends can't have the BMW, the big house, and the fat bank account. Once you succeed, be sure to do your best to reach back and give them a helping hand up the ladder. If you are perceived as giving and helpful despite your "luck," you'll feel much less jealousy from others.

GIVING BACK: MAKING THE WORLD A BETTER PLACE

Helping others achieve the rich life is a matter of seeing the world as a place of abundant opportunities for everyone to succeed rather than a place where there's only so much to go around, only so many pies. I think Louis Barajas has it exactly right when he talks about the way the world really works: "In my belief—and this is the belief of every wealthy and successful person I have ever encountered—there's always enough pie to go around because there's always someone somewhere who's baking more. In truth, the smartest people never spend time worrying about who's got the biggest piece of pie because they're out there building more pie shops! We need to invest in ourselves and our businesses, bringing 'pie shops' of all kinds into the Latino community. . . . When we build our own pie shops, when we create businesses and abundance in our own communities, we can say to each other, 'Be my guest: go ahead and eat the rest of that pie. I know there's another pie coming.'"

Latinas in all walks of life are recognizing that they personally can improve the world they see around them. They do not have to wait to become rich to start turning community problems into solutions, and they do not have to wait to be asked. Money helps, of course, but sometimes all that is necessary is for someone to recognize that some aspect of his or her world could be improved with a little effort. Henry David Thoreau said, "Be not simply good; be good for something."

Until you try it, you can't imagine how good it feels to be good for something, and you can't imagine how much you can get accomplished. No, you can't solve all the world's problems or even all the problems of your community. What you can do is make a big difference in your corner of the world. If enough of us do that, think how much of a difference we can make. Here are a few Latinas who are doing just that as founders, facilitators, board members, and full-time leaders in the nonprofit world.

- *Ysabel Durón, who founded Las Isabelas to improve cancer care for the poor.* Ysabel is a news anchor for KRON in San Francisco who successfully fought cancer six years ago. During her treatment she became acutely aware of the staggering cost of good cancer care and the fact that she was always the only Hispanic person getting care in the advanced clinics she visited. "When you want to avoid dying, you want to find the best care and support, and I discovered that wasn't available to most women in our community," says Ysabel. She started Las Isabelas to provide that support and education locally. By becoming an official nonprofit organization, which is not that hard to do with the help of an experienced accountant, the group was able to raise money, create an educational Web site, and offer a wide range of support services for breast cancer patients in the San Francisco area. Ysabel is hoping to take this education and support effort for Latinas nationwide.

- *Susana Navarro-Valenti, facilitator, who sends computers to México.* "I'm always looking for ways to give back to the Hispanic community," says Susana, who owns Navarro Research and Development, which was the ninth-fastest-growing Hispanic business in the country in 2002. Susana, a nuclear engineer and *mexicana* who came to the United States for graduate school and stayed, worked with the Rotary Club in Oak Ridge, Tennessee, to collect unwanted computers from members and give them to the schoolchildren of Puebla, Mexico, where she once had visited. Susana and her husband also have purchased and outfitted an ambulance for Tepeaca, a Mexican town that had an ambulance "that sometimes started and sometimes didn't." Susana expects no direct benefit for her business from her efforts because the clients of her nuclear and computer-services firm are connected primarily with the U.S. government. It just gives her a good feeling to know she's making the world a better place, one computer (and ambulance) at a time.

- *Kayleen Maya-Avilés, who is a board member of HOPE.* Training Latinas to be tomorrow's political and business leaders is the mission of HOPE (Hispanas Organized for Political Equality), a California-based nonprofit organization that aspires to go national. Kayleen got involved with the group as a result of attending its Leadership Institute. "I came away knowing much more about our culture and believing that any Latina can be a leader," says Kayleen, who is director of public affairs for Valencia, Pérez and Echeveste, a public relations firm in South Pasadena, California. Now, as a board member of HOPE, she is applying her training and skills to motivate other young Latinas to achieve their best and maximize their political power. The group has become powerful enough to attract the participation of California politicians such as Lieutenant Governor Cruz Bustamante and San Francisco Mayor Willie Brown and to be effective in lobbying for legislation to benefit the Hispanic community.

- *Rocío Sáenz, who is president of Service Employees International Union (SEIU), Local 615.* Rocío, an immigrant from Mexico at age 22, became involved in unions when she was trying to find a better job than cleaning houses. By helping office building janitors channel their anger into action in Los Angeles and Boston, she rose to the top post in her local, representing janitors in Massachusetts, Rhode Island, and New Hampshire. Those workers feel particularly isolated because they often work alone in large buildings. Union organizing for such workers must happen building by building, person by person. "If a union is to be the source of hope, it's our responsibility to see that people know about it," she says. In California, Rocío helped build a formidable group to negotiate contracts with business owners, complete with the threat of strikes, called the Justice for Janitors campaign. A three-week strike in Los Angeles persuaded building owners there to take the union seriously. Rocío's style of negotiating—complete with demanding community leaders and lots of noise—has shaken up business as usual in Boston office buildings since she arrived there in 2001. In meetings she's been known to shout out, "*¿Podemos ganar?*" (Can we win?). She now hears the same reply every time: "*¡Sí, se puede!*" (Yes, we can!).

Personally, I am strongly involved in giving back to my community as well. I currently am involved with six charities and eight nonprofit boards. Is that too much? I don't think so. Yes, *mujeres* can and do say *sí* too often when it comes to making commitments to help good causes. Sometimes the worthiness of the cause or the sales ability of the recruiter drags a yes out of us when we don't really mean to say that. And then we find we don't have the energy or, worse, the interest to keep up our end of the bargain. Or we keep our promises but resent every minute of the time those promises take away from other activities that are more important to us. Sound familiar? I'll bet it does. I had a tendency to overcommit myself until I realized that saying yes when I didn't really mean it wasn't helping anyone—good cause or not.

I needed a way to decide what I would commit to, a way to know up front what causes I would be happy working for. Eventually I realized that certain themes repeated themselves in the involvements that lasted for me. (I just realized this could work for dating, too.) I was happiest in charity work that was aimed at educating disadvantaged kids, providing health care for poor uninsured people, and rescuing unwanted pets. The overall theme? Helping those who can't help themselves. It all comes, I think, from a semiconscious desire to help people from backgrounds similar to mine. It's all circles within circles, "paying forward," if you believe the movie that asks us to believe that the good we do in the world will come back to us. I don't believe it happens in that kind of straightforward manner—or else all those good people who are poor through no fault of their own suddenly would become as rich as kings. But I do believe that everything an individual does to

> *It is critical that as we take two steps forward, we bring some Latina women with us.*
>
> Kayleen Maya-Avilés, *board member, Hispanas Organized for Political Equality*

help another creature makes the world around her just that much better.

Think back to the volunteer work you've done, even back when you were a kid. Did you enjoy any of it? What aspects were most enjoyable and why? If you didn't really enjoy organized volunteerism, did some particular acts of kindness that you did or that were done for you make you feel especially good? Try to pick out exactly what it was that caused that feeling in you. What's the common theme in the activities that worked well for you? It could be serving a particular population of the needy. It could be the excitement of being close to power, as in a political campaign. Or it could simply be because it is so different from your daily routine. One woman in Chicago, a public relations consultant, now chairs the fundraising arm of a dance company, among other volunteer commitments. She finds that doing something so different from her day-to-day work gives her an edge in business. "I've made my volunteer work an integral part of my professional life," she said recently. "It definitely keeps me in the loop and helps me maintain the freshness I need for my paying clients."

Right now I'm pursuing a new involvement: helping Hispanic candidates win office. That may not seem to fit in with my theme, but I think it does. Very few Hispanic politicians can raise all the money they need to win without getting a lot of help. Thus, I really am helping those who can't sufficiently help themselves because they aren't independently wealthy and are not willing to sell their souls for the support of corporate fat cats. In politics I've already discovered that both your money and your time can truly make a difference for your chosen candidates. We won't see enough good people in office who look like us until we make the commitment to give of ourselves—and our time—to make it happen.

HAVING THE TIME OF YOUR LIFE

Okay, one last hint. Finding the time to do all the things you need to do personally and professionally to achieve the rich life is not as difficult as it may seem even if you currently have trouble cramming even important things, like your kids' soccer games, into your schedule. Changing the way you cope with life's demands can almost magically diminish your stress level and help you get more of what you want out of life. How can you do this? By slowing down and concentrating on what's meaningful. That's right: slowing down. Despite time management programs that tell us we must be supremely efficient and prioritize our tasks, what I'm suggesting is that you make sure you are busy doing the right things. That means regularly taking the time to step back and question why you are doing any particular task. Continually ask yourself: Will doing this make me happier, even in the long run? If you're doing something for your friends, family, or community that will make others happy and thus lead to your happiness, great. If you're doing something for work that will make someone look upon you more favorably and increase your chances of work satisfaction, great again. If not, why the heck are you doing it?

Cutting out unnecessary tasks will give you the ability to be less frenzied but won't take you far enough down the road to contentment. Along with eliminating the unnecessary things in your life, you need to decide what is missing from your life or what you long for more of. It could be more joy, more love, more time to take hot baths. People who invite a lot of what they desire into their lives are what Seattle psychophysiologist Robert Simon Siegel, the author of *Six Seconds to True Calm*, calls thrivers. Siegel suggests that aspiring thrivers make a list of the feelings that they'd like more of in their lives, and then take some concrete steps to make those things happen. Don't phrase them as problems to be solved or your unconscious mind may throw you back into survival mode. Break them up into small chunks so that you won't have some grand, glorious, and utterly overwhelming goal staring you in the face. That is, rather than "stop procrastinating," try "go to the library to start the research on my book."

Another technique for being more a part of your own life is to keep it in "flow." A fair amount of the tension we feel in everyday life comes from the dreariness of everyday chores that must be done. The problem is that sometimes you'd rather be doing something (anything!) else. Above all, it's the splitting of attention between what you do and what you *want* to do that causes feelings of frustration. A suggestion: Concentrate fully on whatever you are doing, no matter how mundane it is. When you do that, time will seem to disappear, at least for a few moments, and you will enter the peaceful state known as flow. If you have to scrub the sink, don't think about the report that's due tomorrow or the bills. Delight instead in the sensuality of the warm water, contemplate the tree outside the window, or simply be aware of your muscles moving as you work.

This can also be a very effective state of mind when it comes to communicating with kids and other family members. When kids (or husbands) don't seem to be responding to your internally driven time schedule, try matching your time sense to theirs. Try to get into flow with them and you'll be surprised how often conflicts disappear and giggles replace them. Young children in particular respond really well to this effort to be present in the same moment they are. If you can relax into their time and give them your *full* attention for a surprisingly short period, kids—and your *novio*—will tend to wander off contentedly after a while, and that will give you more time for yourself.

But will you be able to use that time well? That depends on whether you are able to get away from your worries and anxieties, especially about work. On average, psychologists tell us, we devote 30 percent of our time to worrying about the future and another 30 percent to replaying the past. Only by remaining in the present moment, the "now," can we silence the voices chattering in our heads. When the chattering gets to be too much, try this: Look at your surroundings and silently name everything you observe, every sound, every smell, without reacting. You can't do this and listen to your internal worrier at the same time. Do this even for a minute and you'll feel more relaxed. And take a "breather" too. You probably are holding your breath or breathing quite shallowly right now because you are concentrating on reading. A few powerful breaths through your nose, deep enough to round your belly, can calm your nerves and greatly improve your ability to cope. It's even more relaxing if you close your eyes while you breathe deeply. Just a couple of breaths will work wonders. You'll see.

Latinas in Congress

- *Lucille Roybal-Allard (D-Calif.)*
- *Grace F. Napolitano (D-Calif.)*
- *Loretta L. Sanchez (D-Calif.)*
- *Elena Ros-Lehtinen (R-Fla.)*
- *Hilda L. Solis (D-Calif.)*
- *Linda Sanchez (D-Calif.)*

FINDING YOUR *VIDA RICA*

No one can tell you whether you'll be successful or rich or happy. I've only tried to pass along what I've learned in my journey from migrant worker to a life I could only dream of out in the fields. I've told you my secrets for success in hopes that you'll use the ones that work for you to find your own path to your dreams. On my path I've learned a few home truths *(verdades caseras)* that might make your way a little brighter.

Truth 1: America Really Is a Land of Opportunity

Anyone who has the desire to better herself can do it—anyone. But the streets are not paved with gold. You must be willing to try anything—and try and try and try. I never got a college education, and I believe that would have helped me a great deal, especially as I was rising in the corporate world. Persistence, though, is even more important. The willingness to come back repeatedly, even bullheadedly, until you get what you want has been the key for me. Yes, America rewards those who help themselves. And this is an especially good time to be a Latina in America because the business world is just waking up to our $2 trillion (!) in annual purchasing power. Help businesses tap into that in some way and you will be a *princesa* who can afford to buy her own glass slippers.

Truth 2: Respect Begins at Home

My *familia* keeps me centered, keeps me real. *Mi mamí* still calls and yells at me if I've been "too busy" to call her, and heaven help anyone who puts on airs at her Sunday brunches. But I've never wanted to be the kind of person who wasn't the same Sunday afternoon as I was Monday morning. Latinas have a strong moral compass that they should take with them into the business world and never be tempted to set aside. If you see things that are wrong, don't be tempted to "go along to get along." That will catch up to you in the end. Business does not need to be done ruthlessly, with only profit in mind. We can help set a different standard merely by speaking our minds. I've always wanted to be able to look in the mirror in the morning and admire the *mujer* I see there.

Truth 3: Lights Shine on Those Who Give Lamps to Others

Perhaps the most precious gift I have been given is the friendship and trust of those I've worked with over the years. I believe I've been able to earn that friendship and trust by allowing those around me to stretch their wings and fly. Never feel that you must prove you know everything because that's impossible to do. If you want to soar to great heights, you must realize that even eagles don't do it on their own. Even they use currents of air to rise to incredible heights. You will too if you surround yourself with smart people and listen to them. Give them credit when an idea of theirs makes you look brilliant or pay them back by finding a way to make them look brilliant in return. You'll create legions of people who will do anything to help you shine.

Truth 4: If You Want to Feel Rich, Count All the Blessings You Have That Money Can't Buy

You can have a rich life without losing your *alma*, your soul. You just have to remember what's important, and that isn't the "stuff" in your life. Living simply, buying only what I really need, keeps me from going crazy over the success that's come into my life. Sure, I can buy nice things now, but I always try to remember that they are just things. You'll never lose your soul in this game if you always realize that it could all be gone tomorrow and learn to believe that that's okay. Then you won't go nuts worrying about things that aren't important in the grand scheme of things.

I'm proud of what I've accomplished. Every day, when I looked in the mirror, even when I was just a dental assistant, I said, "Today is a great day to be alive." And it always was. I believe I have been fair to everyone I've met and have never tried to screw anyone along the way. I tried to learn as much as I could from everyone I met, even bad bosses. I feel I deserve the rich life I have gotten because I worked hard, didn't complain, and helped people coming along behind me. Success could have come to someone else, but I'm truly glad it came to me. If not me, who? You? *¡Absolutamente!* There is no reason in the world why you shouldn't follow in my footsteps. *¡Buena suerte!* Now get to work, *mi amiga*.

For Further Information

Good Reads

Barajas, Louis. *Latino Journey to Financial Greatness: 10 Steps for Creating Wealth, Security and a Prosperous Future for You and Your Family.* New York: HarperCollins, 2003.
A leading financial expert and planner provides advice specifically designed for the problems faced in Hispanic homes.

Bing, Stanley. *Throwing the Elephant: Zen and the Art of Managing Up.* New York: HarperBusiness, 2002.
A fun, Zen-based approach to getting your boss to do what you want.

Bixler, Susan, and Lisa Scherrer Dugan. *Five Steps to Professional Presence: How to Project Confidence, Competence and Credibility at Work.* Avon, MA: Adams Media, 2001.
Good advice, from dressing well and networking confidently to minding your manners and your email.

Deemer, Candy and Nancy Fredericks. *Dancing on the Glass Ceiling: Tap into Your True Strengths, Activate Your Vision and Get What You Really Want Out of Your Career.* New York: McGraw-Hill, 2002.
The advice of two experienced executives on how to break through the glass ceiling and make it to the top of any profession.

Dominguez, Linda. *How to Shine at Work.* New York, McGraw-Hill, 2003.
Filled with top-notch advice from a Latina business consultant.

Fisher, Roger, and William Ury. *Getting to Yes: Negotiating Agreement Without Giving In.* 2nd ed. New York: Penguin, 1991.
The classic book about negotiating, it's less than 100 pages long. Well worth studying.

Glass, Lillian. *I Know What You're Thinking: Using the Four Codes of Reading People to Improve Your Life.* New York: John Wiley & Sons, 2002.
A secret weapon in the power wars.

Heim, Pat and Susan Murphy. *In the Company of Women: Turning Workplace Conflict into Powerful Alliances.* New York: Jeremy Tarcher/Putnam, 2001.
An in-depth look at conflict resolution. A good book to consult if that's a problem in your workplace.

Nelson, Bob. *1001 Ways to Reward Employees.* New York: Workman, 1994.
Some interesting ideas here.

RoAne, Susan. *How to Work a Room: The Ultimate Guide to Savvy Socializing in Person and Online.* New York: HarperResource, 2000.
Another classic, recently revised for the twenty-first century. Excellent advice on networking successfully.

Sanders, Tim. *Love Is the Killer App: How to Win Business and Influence Friends.* New York: Crown, 2002.
How to be an "extreme networker" from the director of Yahoo.com's in-house think tank.

See, Carolyn. *Making a Literary Life: Advice for Writers and Other Dreamers.* New York: Random House, 2002.
Great on the power of thanking people. Also for businesspeople who dream of literary success.

Stanley, Thomas J., and William Danko. *The Millionaire Next Door: The Surprising Secrets of America's Wealthy.* New York: Pocket Books, 1998.
Millionaires are different from the average person—they're tight with a nickel. Interesting insights on the personalities and habits of the average millionaire.

Stanny, Barbara. *Secrets of Six-Figure Women: Surprising Strategies to Up Your Earnings and Change Your Life.* New York: HarperCollins, 2002
One of my new favorite books. Barbara Stanny interviewed dozens of highly paid women for their insights on how to make it big.

Research on Latinas

Catalyst, 120 Wall St., New York, NY 10005, 212-514-7600. Also has offices in San Jose, CA, and Toronto. www.catalystwomen.org
Goal: "Advancing women in business." Research and advice on how women can get ahead . . . and how companies can tap into the talents of their female workforces. Also regularly collects targeted research data about minority women in business, including Latinas.

Pew Hispanic Foundation, Washington, D.C., 202-292-3300, www.pewhispanic.org
The mission of this research organization is to improve understanding of the diverse Hispanic population in the United States and to chronicle Latinos' growing impact on the nation. Women are not separately studied in most of Pew's research projects but the detailed information about our people is enlightening.

Hispanic Association on Corporate Responsibility, www.hacr.org
The HACR works to increase the representation of Hispanics at all levels of corporate activity and strives to make our community more accessible to corporate America, through research and events.

Index

Accented speech, 92–93
Accessories, 160–161
Accountants, 62, 189, 190
Active listening, 96–97
Admiration, 105–106, 120–121
Allowances, 174–176
Appreciation, 85–86, 110–112, 144–145
Asking, importance of, 11–13
Attorneys, 60, 62, 67, 189, 190, 191–192
Attracting positive attention, 92

Bilingual Staffing Solutions, 44
Blame, 77, 79, 93
Blessings, 211–212
Boards of directors, 114–115, 134–135
Body language, 48, 92, 94–95
Brain chatter, 35, 39–42
Budgeting, 173–176
Business cards, 107–108
Business image, 151–167
   achieving rich look in, 157–164
   "don't" list for, 164–167
   getting help with, 154, 163–164, 167
   playing to audience and, 152–157
Business ownership, 70–72
   partners in, 60–61, 62–63
   trends in Latina, 53–54
   (*See also* Risk-taking)

Career selection, 26–46
   career resources, 110–111
   changing jobs, 64–65
   combining passion with work in, 35–38
   finding your passion and, 26–35
   overcoming Internal Critic in, 35, 39–42
   pledging to leave something behind in, 42–46
   responsibility and, 59, 72–74
   (*See also* Risk-taking)
Caring, 85
Casual Fridays, 161
Catalyst, 119, 195
CEO of your own life, 47–74
   business ownership and, 53–54, 70–72
   forward-looking marketing in, 55
   as goal, 47–50
   human resources and, 57–58
   publicity in, 50, 53, 56, 79

CEO of your own life *(Cont.)*:
   quality control in, 52–54
   responsibility and, 59
   saying "no" and, 54
   self-confidence and, 48–49
   steady production in, 51–52
   (*See also* Risk-taking)
Charitable organizations, 113–115, 204–206
Charitable remainder trusts, 191–192
Chewing gum, 166–167
Chores, 197
Clothing (*see* Business image)
Commitment, power of, 43–44, 84
Communication skills, 6, 12, 33, 89–98
   listening, 95–97, 124
   tips for improving, 92–98
Concessions, 66, 67
Conflict resolution, 148–149
Conformity, 7–9, 15–17
   fear of resentment, 40
   lack of self-confidence, 40–42
   macho culture and, 8–9, 13–15, 18, 59, 73–74, 132, 183–188, 198–199
   safety of smallness and, 39–40
   (*See also* Family; Risk-taking)
Confused employees, 89
Consultative selling, 55
Contact management systems, 108, 109, 110
Conversation:
   in deep connecting, 106
   making introductions, 106–107
Courage, 5–7, 82–83
Credit cards, 169, 170–173, 175, 176

Dancing on the Glass Ceiling (Deemer and Fredericks), 97–98
Deadlines, 144
Demographic trends, 9, 18, 134–137, 195
Demoralized employees, 89
Diet, 57–58
Discount shopping, 178–179
Discrimination, 15–17, 134–138
   helpful organizations, 137–138
   prevalence of, 134–137
Disrespecter, 79
Diversification, 183
Divorce, 5, 13–14, 18, 184

E-mail, 108–109, 122
Education, 17–22
   importance of, 17–19
   scholarships for Latinas, 19–22, 49–50
Emergency funds, 175
Energy, personal, 57–58
Enron, 78, 80, 82
Entravision, 3, 10–11, 60–61, 64, 65, 102, 169
Ethical behavior, 140–141
Executive coaches, 140
Exercise, 57–58
Expertise, in risk-taking, 63–64
Eye contact, 48, 94

Fallback plans, 68–69
Family:
   attitudes toward education, 17–19
   creating the life you want, 195–201
   goal-setting in, 196–197
   importance of, 4
   macho culture in, 8–9, 13–15, 18, 59, 73–74, 132, 183–188, 198–199
   money management by, 183–188
   responsibility and, 73–74
   support from, 69–70
   (*See also* Conformity; Risk-taking)
Fear:
   openness and, 87–88, 149–150
   of resentment, 40
   in risk-taking, 67–70, 141–142
Feedback, 77, 86, 89
Feminist movement, 7–9
Firing employees, 88–89
Five Steps to Professional Presence (Bixler), 157
Flirting, 97
Flow, 208
Focus on others, 100, 104–105
Follow-ups, 108–109, 128
Friendship, 103–104, 115–117, 199–201, 211
Full disclosure, 87–88, 146, 149–150, 198

Gestures, 94–95
Get Free Cash for College (Tanabe and Tanabe), 19
Goals:
   flexibility of, 3–6
   production, 51–52
   self-determination and, 47–50
   setting family, 196–197
   setting inspiring, 84
   setting small, 5–7
Golf, 112–113, 122
Grooming, 162

Guilt-free money (GFM), 176
Gut feel, 62–63

Hair care, 162
Handshake, 48, 97
Health insurance, 182
Hiring skills, 83–84
Hispanic Association on Corporate Responsibility (HRAC), 134–136
Hispanic market, 23–24
   (*See also* Demographic trends)
Home ownership, 179–181
Honesty, 79–80, 82, 83–84, 97–98, 132–133
HOPE, 203–204
How to Shine at Work (Dominguez), 139–140
How to Work a Room (RoAne), 105
Hugging, 97
Humor, 34, 92, 128–129, 133–134, 142–143

I Know What You're Thinking (Glass), 94
Image (*see* Business image)
Independence, 144, 197
Inspiration, 75–78, 84
Insults, 128–129
Insurance agents, 190, 191
Internal Critic, 35, 39–42
Interruptions, 131–132
Introductions, 106–107
Intuition, 62–63

Know-Nothing, 79

Lapiz Integrated Marketing, 23
Las Isabelas, 202
Latin Long Island magazine, 28
Latina heritage:
   business ownership and, 53–54
   combining passion with, 28–29
   leadership skills and, 75–78, 81–83, 125–126, 143–150
   making the most of, 23–24
Latino Journey to Financial Greatness, The (Barajas), 200–201
Lazy employees, 88–89
Leadership skills, 75–98
   characteristics of bad bosses, 78–81
   inspiration and, 75–78
   Latina approach to, 75–78, 81–83, 125–126, 143–150
   strategies for developing, 83–91, 143–150
   (*See also* Communication skills)

Index

Liars, 79–80
Life outside work, 142–143, 145–146, 193–212
   creating the life you want, 195–201
   finding your *vida rica*, 210–212
   giving back and, 201–206
   tips for enjoying, 207–209
Listening skills, 95–97, 124
Loans, 70–72
Love Is the Killer App (Sanders), 91

Macho culture, 8–9, 13–15, 18, 59, 73–74, 132, 183–188, 198–199
Makeup, 162, 166–167
Making a Literary Life (See), 111
Male centrality (*see Macho* culture)
Management style, 125–126, 143–150
Marketing, 55
Meetings:
   business image and, 154
   of nonprofit boards, 114–115
Mentoring, 117–124
   being a mentor, 123–124
   business image and, 154, 167
   creating a mentor, 120–122
   importance of, 119
Millionaire Next Door, The (Stanley and Danko), 173–174
Mirrors, 166
Mistakes, 93, 144
Money management, 168–192
   affording risks, 61–62
   attitudes toward, 10–11
   credit cards and, 169, 170–173, 175, 176
   discount shopping and, 178–179
   for families, 183–188
   getting help with, 189–192
   handling raises, 176–178
   home ownership and, 179–181
   risk-taking and, 181–183
   saving and, 169, 175, 176
   for singles, 188–189
   small stuff and, 173–176
Money managers, 190
Morale breakers, 40–42, 146–147
Moving expenses, 65–66, 66
Mutual funds, 182

Nail care, 162
National Hispana Leadership Institute, 77
Navarro Research and Development, 202–203
Negotiation skills, 33
   asking in, 11–13
   within family, 73–74

Negotiation skills *(Cont.)*:
   with partners, 60–61
   responsibility and, 59
   risk-taking and, 65–67
   for salary, 13, 64–66
   written agreements and, 60, 67
Networking (deep connecting), 99–124
   admiration in, 105–106
   appreciation in, 110–112
   conversations in, 106
   focus on others in, 100, 104–105
   following up in, 108–109
   friendship and, 103–104, 115–117
   gathering business cards in, 107–108
   making introductions in, 106–107
   mentoring in, 117–124
   nature of, 100–102
   old-fashioned networking versus, 101
   seeking out powerful people in, 112–115
"No," saying, 54

Office politics, 125–150
   discrimination and, 134–138
   management style and, 125–126, 143–150
   "playing" with men's rules in, 126–134
   power of positive politics and, 139–143
Openness, 87–88, 146, 149–150, 198

Para Me Cosmetics, 162, 167
Participative management, 143–150
Partners, 60–61, 62–63
Passion:
   combining with work, 35–38
   finding, 26–35
Passion Cheat Sheet, 30, 32, 35
Payouts, 60–61, 64
Perfectionism, 73
Performance reviews, 86, 89
Perfume, 162
Pew Hispanic Center, 135
Politeness, 11–13, 131–132
Posture, 48, 92, 158–159
Poverty, 10–11
Power:
   business image and, 152–157
   getting close to office, 127–128
   in networking (deep connecting), 112–115
   of positive politics, 139–143
   of risk-taking, 59–61
Power plays, 130–134
Power position, 65
Power trips, 126–134, 145–146

Praise, 56, 85–86, 105–106, 144–145
Production goals, 51–52
Promises, keeping, 146–147
Promotions, 38, 49, 90
Pronunciation, 92–93
Protecting employees, 86
Publicity, personal, 50, 53, 56, 79
Purses, 161, 165

Quality control, 52–54

Raises, 176–178
Realistic approach:
  to leadership, 85
  in risk-taking, 64–65
Referrals, 106–107, 109
Research:
  on business ownership, 72
  in changing jobs, 64–65
  in negotiation process, 66
  in networking (deep connecting), 104
  on partners, 62
Respect, 4, 79, 81–82, 83, 90, 94–95, 137, 210–211
Responsibility, 59, 72–74, 197
Rest, 57–58
Résumés, 55
Retreat time, 35
Risk-taking, 3, 59–74
  affording, 61–62
  family, 196–197
  fear and, 67–70, 141–142
  importance of, 10–11
  in money management, 181–183
  negotiation in, 65–67
  overcoming Internal Critic and, 35, 39–42
  partners and, 60–61, 62–63
  personal expertise and, 63–64
  pledging to leave something behind, 42–46
  power of, 59–61
  promotions and, 38
  realism and, 64–65
  trust in, 62–63
  (*See also* Business ownership; Career selection; Conformity; Family)
Role models, 83

Salaries:
  high levels of, 45, 136
  negotiating, 13, 64–66
  raises in, 176–178
Saving, 169, 175, 176
Scapegoats, 93

Scarcity syndrome, 200–201
Scholarships, 19–22, 49–50
Secrets of Six-Figure Women, The (Stanny), 45, 136
Security, 87–88, 149–150
Self-confidence:
  acting fearless, 141–142
  body image and, 158–159
  business image and, 152–157
  problems with, 40–42
  signs of, 48–49
Self-employment (*see* Business ownership)
Self-revelation, 124
Service Employees International Union (SEIU), 204
Sexual harassment, 133–134
Shameless Self-Promoter, 79
Shoes, 158, 165–166
Singles, money management by, 188–189
Six Seconds to True Calm (Siegel), 207–208
Sleep, 57–58
Smoking, 166–167
Stockbrokers, 190
Stress management, 57–58
Subconscious mind:
  in finding your passion, 32–33
  self-confidence and, 41
Success:
  challenges for Latinas, 8
  daily opportunities for, 5–7
  image of, 16
  listening skills and, 95–97
  personal definition of, 4, 45–46
  potential roadblocks to, 10–22
Surprises, avoiding, 87–88, 146, 149–150, 198
Symbolic gestures, 93–94

Talents, identifying personal, 29–30
Telemarketing, 101
Thank-you notes, 111–112
Transformational leaders, 125–126
Trust, 62–63, 77, 82, 211

Vacations, 57–58
Viral marketing, 102
Volunteering, 12, 30–32, 113–115, 204–206

"Walk-away," 67
Widowhood, 18
Women's Business Development Centers, 72
Worrying, 57–58, 209
Written agreements, 60, 67

www.ingramcontent.com/pod-product-compliance
Lightning Source LLC
Chambersburg PA
CBHW071437150426
43191CB00008B/1155